ALL LARA'S WARS

ALL LARA'S WARS

WOJCIECH JAGIELSKI

Translated by Antonia Lloyd-Jones

Seven Stories Press
New York • Oakland • Liverpool

This publication has been subsidized by Instytut Książki—
the ©POLAND Translation Program.

Originally published in Polish by Wydawnictwo Znak
under the title *Wszystkie wojny Lary*, 2015.

First English-language edition.

Seven Stories Press
140 Watts Street
New York, NY 10013
www.sevenstories.com

College professors and high school and middle school teachers may order free examination
copies of Seven Stories Press titles. To order, visit www.sevenstories.com or send a fax on
school letterhead to (212) 226-1411.

Book design by Jon Gilbert

Library of Congress Cataloging-in-Publication Data

Names: Jagielski, Wojciech, 1960- author. | Lloyd-Jones, Antonia,
    translator.
Title: All Lara's wars / Wojciech Jagielski ; translated by Antonia
    Loyd-Jones.
Other titles: Wszystkie wojny Lary. English
Description: New York : Seven Stories Press, [2020]
Identifiers: LCCN 2020031054 (print) | LCCN 2020031055 (ebook) | ISBN
    9781644210161 (trade paperback) | ISBN 9781644210178 (epub)
Subjects: LCSH: Chechnya (Russia)--History--Civil War, 1994---Social
    aspects. | Syria--History--Civil War, 2011---Social aspects. | Muslim
    families--Biography. | IS (Organization)--Biography. | Joq'olo
    (Georgia)--History. | Grozny (Russia)--History. |
    Khists--Georgia--Joq'olo.
Classification: LCC DK511.C37 J341513 2020 (print) | LCC DK511.C37
    (ebook) | DDC 956.9104/230923999641--dc23
LC record available at https://lccn.loc.gov/2020031054
LC ebook record available at https://lccn.loc.gov/2020031055

Printed in the USA

9 8 7 6 5 4 3 2 1

Contents

Introduction
7

Map
28

All Lara's Wars
31

Author's Note
253

A Time Line of Events at the Tumultuous
Turn of the Twenty-first Century
255

Translator's Glossary
267

Introduction

Lara missed the old days, when the Kists who lived in the green Pankisi Gorge were never troubled by the question of their identity.

Neither a girl nor an old woman, she tucked some unruly wisps of hair beneath her headscarf. "For at least a hundred years after settling here we were oblivious," she told me. "And why should we have needed to know more?"

Many of the Kists blamed themselves for their own isolation. They so rarely crossed the mountains to visit their kinsmen in Chechnya, on the northern side, that eventually they forgot that anyone lived there at all. But in the distant past, that was where they had lived too, before migrating south. Now they wondered if they'd done well to rediscover the far side of the mountains and the big city lying beyond it. Opinion in the gorge was divided, and by no means did everyone share Lara's view. Some thought the misfortunes she had suffered were influencing her speech—anyone feeling such awful pain is bound to yearn for the past.

There were some who claimed they'd always been aware of their northern, Chechen origins. Ali, Lara's younger cousin, insisted he'd always known he was a Chechen. Lara and the other locals would smile indulgently and say he could remember no such thing. Of course they knew the old legends of how the Kists had come to the gorge across the mountains from Chechnya, but very few of them had ever set eyes on a Chechen before.

"There were all sorts of stories about them," said Lara. "About how wonderful, how rich and valiant they were. But all we really knew was that they existed, they were Muslims like us, and they lived on the other side of the mountains—where exactly, very few of us were sure. Hardly anyone crossed over the mountains, because there was no reason to. So in fact it was impossible to say anything certain about them. To us, they were a bit like characters from a children's fairy tale."

Although few people in the gorge had endured as much or suffered as much pain as she had, Lara never complained about her fate or the injustice done to her. She never paraded her misfortune or sought sympathy or consolation. The only time I ever heard a mild hint of grievance in her voice was when she was telling me about the plight of the entire Pankisi Gorge and its Kist inhabitants. And she was one of them—born, raised, and spending most of her life in this valley deep among the great canyons of the Caucasus.

For at least a century, maybe two, the Kists hadn't given any thought to their origins, though they knew perfectly well where their ancestors had come from. They'd all heard the stories passed down through the generations about the migrants who had crossed to the southern slopes of the Caucasus Mountains over two hundred years ago and found shelter among the Georgian princes living there.

The princes had welcomed them with open arms and entertained them royally, in typical Georgian style. And then, in a sudden surge of emotion—nothing unusual at a Georgian feast, where the table groans with food and there's a cup of young wine in every hand—they informed the newcomers that if they liked it here in this green valley, they could stay forever. They'd be given land for new farms, vegetable plots, gardens, and orchards, and they'd be able to graze their flocks on the highland pastures. The newcomers silently exchanged glances and, without needing to confer, agreed that they'd never find a better life than here. So they decided to settle in the gorge.

And no wonder, because there was no finer place on earth. The Georgian principality of Kakheti was like paradise. It lay in a flat basin, fenced off from the outside world by mountains that protected it from storms and severe winters, while the rivers and streams flowing from the rocky hillsides amply watered the local fields and pastures. The result was an abundant harvest of all sorts of crops, fruits and vegetables, succulent grass, flowers, and fragrant herbs, many of which had healing powers.

But for centuries, Kakheti's riches—or, rather, legends about how copious and splendid they were—had attracted terrifying invaders eager to steal its wealth. With fire and sword, the Mongol horde of Genghis Khan, Tamerlane's troops, and the Persian and Turkish armies had all rolled through Kakheti, leaving no stone standing. Not even the neighboring tribes, the Avars and Lezgins, could resist the temptation to rob the Kakhetians and kidnap the famously beautiful Georgian women; nor could other looters from the Azerbaijani khanates. At last, the powerful Russians invaded from the north.

The strong stone walls, moats, and defensive towers the Kakhetians had built around their towns, villages, and churches were of no use at all. The constant attacks and invasions devastated Kakheti, reducing it to ruins again and again. Finally, the land was in such decline that the local princes decided to bring in warlike highlanders and give them land in exchange for their acting as guardians of the region, defending it against invaders. Exempt from the taxes and obligations mandatory for the common subjects, these men were to come forward at every summons, including if one of the Georgian kings decided to go to war abroad.

The kings didn't have to wait long for the new arrivals to start coming down to Kakheti from the highlands. The Kists were not the only race to be tempted by the promise of a life of plenty in the sunshine.

The first to respond to the call of the Kakhetian princes were their kinsmen, the Georgian highlanders. They had the shortest journey to make and were given a warm welcome. So were the Khevsurians, who wore costumes resembling chain mail, which they customarily decorated with the sign of the cross. As a result, and also because of their great bravery and love of every kind of weaponry, the Khevsurians were said to be descended from medieval knights who had lost their way on the journey home from the crusades to the Holy Land and had chosen to settle in the Caucasus.

As soon as they heard that the Kakhetian princes were distributing land to highlanders, people started arriving from all directions—Armenians, Azeris, Jews, Russians, Greeks, and Ossetians. There were even fearless Lezgins and fierce

Avars, highland warriors who prompted terror throughout the Caucasus.

There were also Chechens, the Kakhetians' neighbors from the northern side of the mountains, who came from the vast gorges along the Argun River. Living in such a remote place, cut off from the outside world, may have given them a sense of security, but life there wasn't easy. Their highland wilderness guarded them against their enemies, and so did the stone towers that they built on the mountainsides. They could not only see approaching danger from these structures, but they could also shelter behind their fortified stone walls. Supplied with food and water, they could defend themselves from inside the towers until their attackers, wounded and disheartened, finally sounded the retreat. But even when the enemy had withdrawn, and daily life among the Caucasian peaks was free from fear and danger, it didn't assume color, vigor, and flavor—this was no land of milk and honey. Especially during the severe winters, when snowstorms closed the passes, and the Argun River and the mountain streams froze solid, changing their waters into figures of ice, like dragons and palaces from ancient legends. Life demanded constant effort and sacrifice, and was reduced to an endless struggle to survive, one where the victor's only laurels were the opportunity to face the next battle. No wonder that on hearing of the Kakhetian princes' invitation, the Chechens were happy to abandon their hardships and head south across the mountains. The mere thought of such a great change in their lives gave them joy.

The invitation came at the right time, because war had come to the Chechen *auls*—the Caucasian word for "fortified villages"—on the northern side of the mountain range; the vicious, merciless fighting seemed endless. Russia, the superpower to the north, had already occupied Georgia; after settling on the southern slopes of the Caucasus, it had decided to conquer the northern ones too. Some of the Chechens joined the insurgents, who were determined not to let the Russians into their part of the Caucasus, but who wanted to set up their own state in the mountains, where they would rule and live according to the Koran. Others chose to escape, not just from the Russians' punitive expeditions and the horrors of the war—which was to continue for half a century—but also from the strict law and order established by the insurgents in the mountains.

After the region was conquered by Russia and became a more peaceful place, the Chechens continued to be attracted to sunny, comfortable Kakheti by the desire to get rich, to rise above others, and to be free of the confining bonds of their community, or at least to loosen them. This was because the law in force among them, passed down from one generation to the next, obliged them to share the pastureland, watering holes, and privately owned ponds, allowing nobody to have more than the rest, so that their community would never descend into serfdom, exploitation, and tyranny. The village elders enforced these rules. If they noticed that any member of the community was acquiring wealth that they regarded as excessive, they would hold a special meeting, then remove the rich man's extra property and share it among the rest, to each according to his needs.

Those who wanted to have more than the others, perhaps more than they actually needed, left for Kakheti, where no one was going to stop them or condemn them for it. In the broad green valley they could have as much property as they wanted. No one would accuse them of having a weakness for comfort and luxury; no one would assess their wealth or insist they share it. On the contrary, here their prosperity prompted admiration, and if it also stirred envy, that was just another reason to feel satisfied, confirmation of the success they had achieved.

There were others who fled across the mountains not in pursuit of an easier or better life, but in order to survive. They came to escape the vengeance sworn against them by their own neighbors, who were not just their compatriots but quite often their blood relatives too. According to local law in the mountains, death or wounding could only be avenged by the killing or injuring of the perpetrator, and if anyone committed a crime of this kind, his entire family was considered culpable. The penalty for death was death, and it was the sacred duty of the victim's sons, brothers, and other relatives to take revenge. Failing to comply with this law brought disgrace on the entire family and made it a laughingstock for centuries.

The indigenous Georgian population of Kakheti named the new settlers Kists. Apparently they couldn't pronounce the name these Chechens from the upper branch of the Argun used to define themselves. The name they used was "Kiist-khoy," which in the Chechen language means, roughly, "people from the land by the gates." Neither Lara, nor her friend and contemporary Omar, nor her cousin Ali, the youngest of them, was able to explain what gates their ancestors were thinking of when they chose this name for their *teip* (a community united not so much by blood ties as by the fact that its members inhabit the same territory, usually on hillsides or at the foot of a mountain). Omar thought the name referred to their land's close proximity to heaven, at the very gates of paradise. Higher up, above their farms and pastures, there was nothing but the rocky, unconquered peaks of the Caucasus reaching to the stars. Lara shook her head and insisted that the name was more likely to have come from their proximity to Kakheti, which lay just beyond the Caucasus range, in its southern foreland. Among all the Chechen communities from the northern side, the Kist villages were closest to Georgia. That must have been the origin of the "gates" in their name. But the Georgian Khevsurians, who had lived along the border for centuries, twisted "Kiistkhoy" and simply called them Kists.

However, according to historians, the Kists took their name from their former settlement to the north of Mount Kirolam, beyond a deep valley that led in a single day's walk to Khevsureti, on the Georgian side. The settlement was on a mountain stream, and its name was Aul Kii. In the language of its inhabitants, the word *kii* meant "water," and *ist* meant "riverbank." This would imply that the Kiistkhoy were not the "people from the land by the gates," but the "people living on the riverbank."

For their new farms, the Georgian princes assigned them the Pankisi Gorge, six miles long and three miles wide, tucked in between the mountains and bisected by the Alazani River, which flows down the Caucasian slopes and is supplied by melting snows and glaciers.

The Kists were not the first settlers in the Pankisi Gorge. Some of the Georgian highlanders whom the Kakhetian princes had rewarded with land in gratitude for their brave and loyal military service had come to live here before them. The Georgians had built their own villages on the left bank of the river, so the new arrivals spread out along the right bank.

In their new location, among new neighbors, the Kists didn't feel like outsiders. They had known the Georgian highlanders for centuries. The two had lived on either side of the same boundary, across the mountains from each other. They had had a few wars, but had mostly lived in peace, visiting each other's villages, making friends, and accepting one another. Sometimes Chechens had adopted Georgians as members of their clans, and vice versa, and they had intermarried too. They had formed brotherhoods, shared their joy at weddings and their grief at funerals. They even had the same pagan gods, whom they worshipped in a similar way.

This didn't change when Christianity and Islam reached the Caucasian ravines. While the Georgians to the south became Christians, and the Chechens to the north became Muslims, they didn't regard each other as enemies. Although they prayed differently now, and in separate temples, they preserved similar customs and the same old love of feasting, the same food and wine. They also remained loyal to many of their old common beliefs, though from now on they kept them secret from outsiders, for fear of being seen as pagans and barbarians.

In their ravines high in the mountains, they continued to celebrate the old festivals together, make pilgrimages to the sacred sites, and honor the gods of fire and nature by making sacrifices to them and placing themselves in their care. Nor did they see anything wrong with attending rites of worship as welcome guests at the temples of either denomination.

According to Caucasian legend, all the highland tribes were descended from a common ancestor, Targamos, a descendant of Japheth, one of the three sons of Noah, who escaped the flood by building an ark that came to rest on Mount Ararat. According to the biblical story, Japheth was the father of all the peoples of the North.

In their new home in the Pankisi Gorge, the Kists lived in clover, among good neighbors and even better nature. Just as in the past, when they lived along the Argun, here too they herded sheep and made occasional trips into the mountains to hunt wild animals in the dense forests.

They despised farming, regarding digging in the earth as beneath a man's dignity; men were destined to be heroes, warriors, conquerors, or, in the worst case, martyrs. They left the farmwork to the women, and many years had to go by, and a lot had to happen, before they started to change their views. But even today, Kist women are a more common sight in the fields along the Pankisi Gorge; the men prefer to keep bees and tend domestic vineyards.

Their new life was so similar to the old one that, gradually, the Kists forgot they'd ever lived anywhere except the Pankisi Gorge. As the move had changed so little, and hadn't demanded any sacrifice, they forgot about it very quickly, just as they forgot everything that came before it. As their memories faded, they grew more and more rooted in the gorge, regarding it as their real home, their true place on earth.

And gradually their trips north to visit their Chechen brothers became rarer. The mountain ranges separating the Chechen ravines from Georgian Kakheti and the Pankisi

Gorge seemed to grow higher and mightier. The journey began to seem too long and too difficult, and there was always something preventing them from traveling. They were also put off by the Russians, who had conquered the entire Caucasus range, including the lands to the north and south of it. As the new rulers of Kakheti and all Georgia, the Russians discouraged the local inhabitants from making unnecessary journeys, multiplying the obstacles in the belief that the less the Kists knew about life beyond the Pankisi Gorge, the less trouble they would cause them. Immobilized, tied to the land, they wouldn't even know they'd been enslaved.

Separated from their Chechen compatriots and living among Georgians, the Kists became more and more Georgian. They learned the Georgian language, became familiar with Georgian customs, and adopted many as their own. They sent their children to Georgian schools, where they learned about Georgian history, Georgian kings, heroes, and poets. Some of the Kists even adopted the Christian faith practiced by the Georgians, some out of genuine conviction, others for the sake of peace and quiet. Yet others were forced to convert to the new faith by Russian soldiers and Christian priests who, one fine day, simply herded the Kists to the Alazani River and, without asking how they felt about it, baptized them in its waters and gave them Christian names.

The Kists took on Georgian surnames and were given Georgian nationality and passports. Soon they were so well integrated that they began to think of themselves as one of the Georgian highland ethnicities, like the Svans, Khevsurians, and Tushs. This new, acquired identity saved them from being exiled from the Caucasus to Kazakhstan, a fate to which Joseph Stalin, himself a native of Georgia, condemned all other Chechens, whom he suspected of disloyalty.

The Kists escaped not just wartime exile, but all the other historic upheavals that rolled across the world, changing its shape and order. Indeed, the news that came from afar was so unusual that they found it hard to believe. Enclosed by the Caucasus Mountains, they heard about regicides, revolutions, and great wars, none of which had access to their godforsaken valley, but simply passed it by.

In Tbilisi, the governors appointed by the Russian tsars were replaced by Georgian prefects, but they too were soon replaced by new administrators from the Kremlin, who demanded to be called "comrades" and "secretaries," and who claimed that all people were equal and alike. They also said there was no God, so the mosques and Orthodox churches would have to close; the buildings would be more useful as stores and preschools.

But the Kists weren't interested in politics, and there were only a handful of them, just a few thousand, in half a dozen villages, so their life in the Pankisi Gorge continued at its own pace, without much change. Only once in a while, armed insurgents would come down from their mountain hideouts to the shepherds' huts on the pastures. These rebels against injustice roamed the Caucasian ravines and passes, and came to the Kists, who knew the mountains inside out, to have them serve as guides and to seek their hospitality and shelter for the winter.

But Stalin's successors failed to maintain the sinister super-power that occupied Europe and Asia from the Baltic to the

Sea of Japan and from the Arctic to the Hindu Kush and Pamir Mountains. Dubbed the Evil Empire, the Soviet Union, in control of half the world and keeping the other half in constant fear, collapsed in ruins like all its predecessors.

So recently paralyzed by fear, one after another of the Soviet Union's servile provinces shook off their impotence and declared independence. One of these was Georgia, and a hundred years after recognizing themselves as Georgians, its Kist citizens, to their own surprise, rediscovered their Chechen heritage.

For many years, the Caucasian highlanders, especially the Chechens, had been traveling far into Russia in search of work—to the Volga Region, to Saint Petersburg in the north, and to Moscow, but also as far as the Urals and even Siberia. But for the Kists, who now began to head after them, even the Chechen capital Grozny, built by the Russians as their greatest stronghold in the Caucasus, was a wonder.

They were amazed by its size and wealth, its refineries and large factories that provided the jobs and income that were lacking in the Pankisi Gorge. They were also filled with pride that the Chechens, their blood relatives, had achieved such splendors.

As poor cousins from a remote provincial backwater, the Kists couldn't stop admiring the greatness of Grozny, and as they feasted their eyes on it, they felt it rubbing off on them. They rose in their own estimation, and thought others were starting to regard them with greater respect, or even admiration.

They felt rather ashamed of failing to go see the Chechens until poverty began to grind them down in Georgia. And of failing to renew their kinship sooner, when they had lived in the same country, ruled by the Russians, but had only started to visit once the state border between Russia and Georgia separated them. The northern, Chechen mountainsides were now on the Russian side, and the southern ones were part of Georgia. But that didn't bother the Kists much—they were used to life in the mountains, where the real borders were drawn by mountain passes and peaks, not by lines on maps.

They were delighted to discover that the Chechens, the most populous and powerful ethnic group in the northern Caucasus, spoke the same language they did, prayed the same way, had the same customs, and were generally similar to them. *So, we're Chechens!* the Kists exclaimed with joy, though it was tempered by the bitter thought that they were turning their backs on the Georgians, showing ingratitude to the people who had once taken them in.

And the Georgians did feel betrayed, especially since the Chechens had fought for their enemies, the Abkhazians, in one of the many wars that erupted in the Caucasus following independence, helping them to inflict a humiliating defeat on the Georgians.

In that period following the collapse of the Soviet Empire, all its former subjects were asking themselves the questions "Who exactly are we? And who are we not?," "What makes us different from others?," "Who should give precedence to whom?," and "Whose blood is better?"

The sudden urge to look for their roots and discover their identity prompted a new wave of migration. Some Kists returned home, while others took to their heels to run as fast and as far as possible from places where they were seen as enemies and traitors.

Nobody drove anyone out of the Pankisi Gorge, but even there, at the end of the world, people began leaving to live among their own ethnicity, to have cousins and compatriots as their neighbors.

The Ossetians, who had also fought a war against the Georgians, moved away. Others, including Tushs, Pshavs, and Khevsurians, went to live closer to their own people too. As a result, the Kists were left with almost sole possession of the entire Pankisi Gorge, though they too began to journey north across the Caucasian ridge in greater numbers, to join the Chechens.

Seeing them setting off, the Georgians ceased to regard them as their countrymen. But their Chechen brothers didn't welcome them with open arms at all—they didn't see them as their equals, but as rather primitive distant cousins.

Even so, the Caucasian wave of migration seemed endless. Fueled by a longing for freedom, by hatred, and by the wars that had broken out in new locations or at the sites of old battles that had only just calmed down, the Caucasian highlanders were driven from north to south and from east to west.

Then the biggest of all the wars in the Caucasus erupted in Chechnya, where, following the example of the Georgians, the people announced that they wanted to live in their own state too, and declared their independence. The two major wars that rolled through Chechnya almost consecutively at the turn of the twenty-first century razed the rebellious country and decimated its population. Refugees came flooding out of the Caucasus in all directions, and the Kists who'd been lured to Grozny by its bright lights and prosperity went back across the mountains to the peaceful Pankisi Gorge, counting on the Georgians to forgive them rather than slam the door in their faces. The Georgians didn't harbor any grudges, and they took the wanderers in. In the wake of the Kists, thousands of Chechens crossed the mountains into Georgia too. Now that they were in need, they were willing to acknowledge their kinship with their forgotten cousins.

The small gorge became a crowded place. At one point there were more newcomers from Chechnya than local Kists, and the Georgians began to complain that Pankisi and the vicinity was no longer part of Georgia, but had become a new province of Chechnya.

Gradually, the Chechen insurgent commanders who, by hiding among civilians, had slipped across the mountains to lick their wounds, gather strength, and muster new troops on the Georgian side, were taking control of the gorge. With them came their mullahs, who taught that solidarity in faith should take precedence over blood ties and that the martyr's war for salvation was more important than the fight for freedom. And with the mullahs came Muslim volunteers. As soon as they'd heard about the war in the Caucasus, they had declared it a holy war and poured in from all over the world to do their religious duty by taking part in it and, if Allah proved merciful, dying as martyrs for their faith, thus achieving salvation.

Once they had made themselves at home among the Kists, regardless of good manners, the mujahideen (as the foreign fighters were called) and the Chechen mullahs and insurgents began to reprimand their hosts for not knowing the Koran or its laws and for failing to observe them; they said it was understandable but unforgivable that the Kists didn't live as Allah decreed and didn't even know the right way to pray to Him.

They couldn't accept that the Muslims who lived in the Pankisi Gorge drank wine and paid occasional visits to their Christian neighbors' churches. "You believe in sorcery and old wives' tales! You live like pagans!" they complained. "Enough! It's high time you mended your ways!"

Annoyed by the outsiders' bad manners, the older Kists refused to hear a word of it. But to the young men, who were fed up with their fathers' and grandfathers' strict and ruthless control, the mullahs' appeal for recognition of the true faith and the road to salvation offered a chance to loosen the bonds restraining them and gain more freedom.

The Georgians had their sights fixed on distant Europe and even more distant America—on their wealth, their almost unlimited freedom, their relaxed morals verging on dissolution, and especially their sacred, almost universal ban on banning anything. So they too were encouraging the young Kists to choose liberty and rebel against their elders.

At the time, the prevailing belief, especially in the West, was that political systems of the European kind were humanity's highest achievement and that they could be introduced anywhere, to the benefit of all—in Siberia or the Sahara, in the Hindu Kush, the Arabian Desert, the Congolese jungle, or at the heart of Africa. Surely it would be easy to recreate Europe in the Caucasus, which wasn't so far away? "We're going to live just as they do in New York, Berlin, and Paris," said the Georgians. "We only have to copy them, try to be like them, try to be Europeans. So if you are Georgians—and you are, because you live in our country—you're Europeans too, just like us."

"Yes, we are!" the young Kists agreed excitedly.

"It doesn't matter if you're Kists, Chechens, or Georgians. First and foremost, you're Muslims, and that's all that counts," the bearded mullahs and pilgrims from Arabia whispered in their other ear. "The West has renounced its god; the Western god is dead. But Allah is great. *Allahu akbar!* In the name of God! *Bismillah!* Don't let yourselves be tempted by the lure of Satan, do not stray from the right path. Don't commit sin, don't do evil, but think of your salvation."

Those Kists who believed they were Europeans were obliged to fight alongside the Georgians in another war against the Russians, who had always been annoyed by the Georgians' superiority and Western fantasies. Meanwhile, the Kists who listened to the god-fearing imams first went to study at Muslim academies in Arab capitals and then joined the holy war as mujahideen, to fight in the battles for Baghdad, Mosul, Damascus, and Aleppo. "Perhaps we condemned ourselves to this eternal wandering?" said Lara. "If you leave your appointed place on earth and go off in search of a better life somewhere else, surely you bring a curse on yourself that means you'll be drifting forever, endlessly looking for something you're never going to find?"

She also said that although she couldn't remember where she first read it, for some strange reason she'd never forgotten the following sentence: "A tribe that's doomed to one hundred years of solitude will never have a second chance." That was the gist of it, though she wasn't sure if it came from an old legend or from one of the novels she used to love reading. Or perhaps it was from a history book or a stage play?

She found it frustrating that she couldn't easily cast her mind back to the old days and move around in the past at will, exploring the recesses of earlier events. "It's all nonsense! Ancient history!" she'd say in despair. "I've lost the habit of reading. But I haven't forgotten that sentence: 'A tribe that's doomed to one hundred years of solitude will never have a second chance.' Sometimes I think it could be about us. Because what can you say about someone who takes a whole century to start wondering who he really is? Perhaps all you can say is that he has lost or denied his identity and spent all that time being nobody. You can understand why he lacks certainty or faith; he feels inferior, so he tries to be like those who've outclassed him. He doesn't try to catch them up, just to copy them. And even when he finally achieves his aim, he can't rejoice, because he doesn't know what he owes his victory to. Did we need that? What good has searching for ourselves brought us?"

Feeling himself to be a Georgian and a European, a young Kist from the next village who was an old friend of Lara's cousin Ali and had also been to school with her sons had joined the Georgian army. He had completed training in Europe and in America with distinction, was promoted to the rank of officer, and fought bravely in the war against the Russians. But after the war, the Georgians had excluded him from their society. He claimed they had brought false charges against him, stripped him of his rank, expelled him from the army, and thrown him in jail like a common criminal.

On his release, like some of the other Kists, he went away to work in Turkey, where he heard about the war that had broken out across the border in Syria. Like earlier wars fought in Palestine, Kashmir, Afghanistan, Bosnia, the Caucasus, and Iraq, the conflict in Syria was soon declared a jihad, a holy war. Not just to earn a living, but also to have an adventure, and for lack of anything better to do, he enlisted with the mujahideen army fighting to establish "God's first righteous caliphate," or Islamic State, which was to encompass Damascus, Baghdad, and all the territory inhabited by Muslims.

The young man distinguished himself so highly in fighting for the caliphate that he soon became one of its leading emirs, as their commanders are called. His fame prompted other Kists to copy his example. As everyone in the Pankisi Gorge knew everyone else, and they always helped one another, they were used to the idea that wherever they went, they could count on the support of a cousin or a countryman. So when they heard about the successful career their compatriot had made in the caliphate, they set off for Syria too, counting on their friend the emir not to leave them in poverty but to lead them to great victories, guaranteeing them wealth and immortal glory.

Lara's cousin Ali was one of the Kists who went to Syria, though by his own admission, his main reason for joining the mujahideen was to escape crushing poverty and the overwhelming sense of hopelessness that was making his life seem pointless.

Lara's sons went to Syria too, to do their religious duty by fighting in the holy war and to earn salvation as mujahideen. And Lara headed after them, to save them from misfortune and death, even if it was the martyr's kind that opened the gates of paradise. She was sure she could persuade them that they must live, not die.

Omar would certainly have gone to Syria too, if he hadn't already lost his faith in war, in life, and even in death.

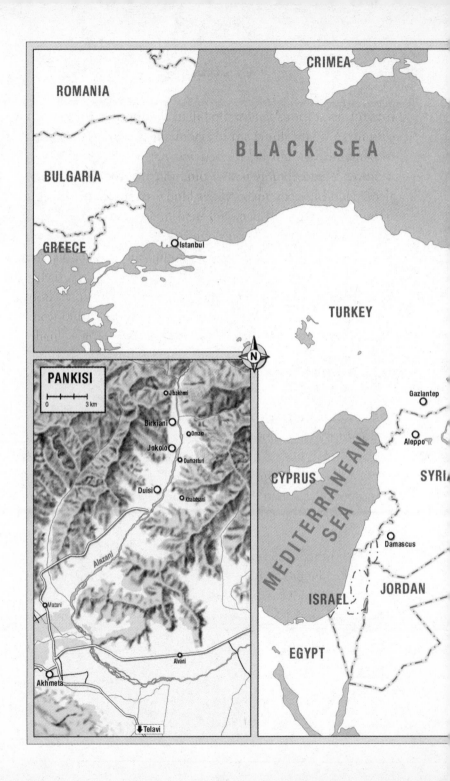

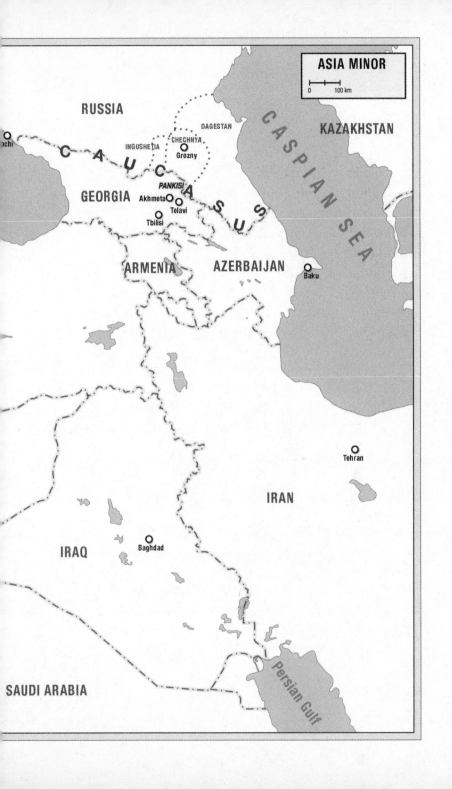

All Lara's Wars

"I am Lara. I don't know what else to say about myself."

In a sky-blue headscarf and a full ankle-length skirt, she looked like a village woman who had interrupted her work in the fields for a break and a chat with her neighbors.

She didn't fit in the big city and looked completely out of place in McDonald's, which is where she had chosen to meet me. In fact, I don't know if there was anywhere on earth that was the right place for her at this moment.

"Where should I start? And how am I to organize it all? Where's the beginning, and where's the end? I don't know anymore." Automatically, she tidied her hair, which kept escaping waywardly from under her headscarf. "I've been such a long way. I thought it would never end."

She had a ponderous figure and the face of a grieving woman crushed by fate, one who just needs to rest. But life burned brightly in her eyes and in her voice, with a youthful, lively flame, leaving no room for bitterness or doubt. She said she was overwhelmed by exhaustion, but as she spoke, you only had to look away to be under the illusion that she was a traveler complaining about the hardships of a journey but looking forward to the road ahead, to surmounting the next obstacles and conquering the next impossible peaks. Anyone who heard Lara's tale and followed her along the uneven paths of her life fell under this illusion.

"The weather's turned cold," she said, rubbing her hands together and adjusting her scarf under her chin. "Any moment now it'll be winter."

The day before, the season's first cold rain had fallen here in Tbilisi; in the night, the wind had torn the last leaves from the trees, tossing them at the feet of the huddled pedestrians and into the headlights of the cars on the downtown avenues. That morning, the radio news had reported snowfall in the Caucasian Mountains; apparently the bad weather might last for several days, at least until the end of the week.

From the ground floor of the restaurant came a shy but ever-louder buzz of voices, and the odors of hot oil and coffee drifted up from the kitchen. "Hamburger and double fries, please! Two chocolate shakes!" But upstairs, where we were sitting, it was still quiet and empty, and the freshly washed floor smelled of soap.

I wondered why she had chosen the McDonald's fast-food restaurant as our meeting place. Here, like everywhere else on earth, most of its customers were young people, noisy, impatient, and avid for life.

I knew Lara was familiar with the city, but she didn't seem to frequent any of the cafés specializing in Georgian cuisine, those places where people looked down on McDonald's as an American intruder. Anyone who arranged to meet at a Georgian restaurant had to be ready to spend a long time there. The food took longer to prepare, no meal was limited to just one or two courses, and the age-old feasting ritual required patience. It wasn't appropriate to leave the table suddenly, excusing yourself with an urgent phone call or other emergency. But the fast-food place imposed no rules and no ceremony. Instead, it guaranteed anonymity and the chance of an instant getaway under any pretext. A few mouthfuls of food, a few sips of tea or coffee, and you could say goodbye and leave without attracting anyone's attention.

Maybe that was what she needed? Maybe she wanted to be sure she could break off her story and end the meeting at any point, if the talking proved beyond her strength? Or perhaps McDonald's was just closest to where she was staying in Tbilisi before traveling onward?

She didn't want to eat or to order anything.

"A cup of tea, perhaps?" I said.

"Tea? Well, all right, perhaps I will." She stared into space. "Tea will do me good. Yes, please."

When I came back with the cardboard cups, she was sitting just as I had left her, in the same pose, with the same absent look on her face. She can't have budged at all.

As I was searching for the right words, she opened the conversation herself.

"When I lost my husband, and then both my brothers were killed, I thought war was a man's business, and women had no part in it. But I refused to give up my sons. I was their mother; my right to them was greater." War was like a curse that had dogged her at every step, constantly reminding her of its presence and steadily robbing her of everything she loved or valued. "I followed them abroad, across Turkey and all the way to the Arabian Desert, to beg them to come home to me. To tell them they belonged to me, their mother, and owed me obedience. But they refused to listen. I had my ideas, and they had theirs. They kept saying it was their destiny to die a martyr's death, which would give them salvation. And they told me to go home. I did, because where else could I go? What else could I do with myself? Like it or not, until death comes for you, you have to go on living. Even if you feel there's nothing left to live for and you're praying for death. So I went home."

Lara's home was in the village of Jokolo, one of seven scattered along the Pankisi Gorge, the valley bisected by the Alazani River. Originally, the villages had been far apart, separated by meadows, but over time they'd expanded, running wild and occupying every free scrap of land. Today, only the oldest residents can tell where one village ends and the next begins.

The Pankisi villages lie on either side of the river and the road that runs along it, connecting the gorge with the rest of Kakheti. This is fertile land, the source of Georgia's finest wines and sweetest grapes, juiciest apples, cherries, watermelons, and melons, best nuts, maize, and tobacco. There were gnarled fruit trees in Lara's orchard in the village of Jokolo, and grapevines covered the trellis her father had set up around the house, including over the wide porch and the balconies. In summer, a dense, living roof of dark-green leaves provided pleasant shade, a refuge from the burning hot sun. It also offered protection from the warm rain and storms that came rolling over the craggy mountains clearly visible from here.

The house where Lara was born and raised was large and spacious, with several stories, like all houses in the Caucasus. They needed to be large enough not just for the local highland families, consisting of several generations, but also for visiting relatives, guests, and passing travelers—sheltering visitors was a sacred duty in the mountains. Lara's family home was at the edge of the village, far from the road, on a slope covered with tall grass, among pastures and colorful meadows where Lara and her siblings had played as children.

There were six of them: first, four girls, and finally, two boys, born when Lara's father was already losing hope of a son and heir.

They lived poorly, but no better or worse than anyone else in the village. The villages in the gorge were never affluent, and apart from herding sheep and tending vegetable plots, gardens, and orchards, there were few other occupations here. Those who remained in the gorge were willing to live as their fathers and grandfathers had before them, according to the same rules and values that had been in force for years, following in the footsteps of previous generations. The few who decided to abandon their customary life and go abroad to make their living hardly ever returned.

As she was growing up, Lara never imagined a life outside the gorge. She had all she needed here. Everything here was to her liking, everything was in its place, and there was nothing she wanted to change. She liked her home, which was always neat and full of life; she liked the layout of the rooms and the furnishings, even the modest rugs on the walls and the curtains on the windows. She liked its constancy, and to keep it that way, she was happy to help her mother with the housework. She also liked to sit on the porch and gaze down at the Alazani River as it came pouring from the steep slopes of the rocky Caucasus, suddenly lost speed in the gorge, spilled into shallow meanders, and then flowed onward, downward, right across Kakheti, watering the local vineyards, orchards, gardens, and fields. As children, they went to bathe in it in summer, and floated down it on inner tubes. The bravest children would climb up riverside boulders and leap into the water, showing off their agility and daring. The older boys sometimes headed up the river to catch trout, which they baked on campfires in the evenings. Though by day it was rapid and burbling, after dusk or in cloudy weather the water in the Alazani seemed to curdle, taking on the look and color of lead.

From the porch on a fine day, Lara also had a clear view of the faraway peaks of the Caucasus. Her father taught her to recognize Tebulos, the highest mountain in the region, marking the border between Georgia and Chechnya.

As she scanned the mountains in the distance, Lara liked to gaze at the dense forest that covered them. Especially in the fall, when the oak and beech trees, the hornbeams and chestnuts, took on yellow, gold, and copper-red colors, a hundred shades of brown and purple. At this time of year, the farmwork came to an end with the harvest of grapes, nuts, and sweet chestnuts, for which the villagers went high into the mountains, as far as the Batsara nature reserve, where they sometimes crossed paths with wild goats, lynxes, wolves, and bears.

Early fall was Lara's favorite time of year. First the school term began, which as a little girl she had always looked forward to. She liked to study, and she liked the daily routine of lessons that followed a set timetable, which nothing and nobody could change or cancel.

She liked the early fall, when the days were still warm and bright, because it brought pleasant variety after the monotony of the long, hot summer vacation. Although Lara wasn't fond of change, she found idleness even more unbearable.

Apart from school, the fall heralded important, much-anticipated events in the gorge that occurred every year in their own special season. The last crops were gathered in from the vegetable gardens and orchards, and two-wheel carts drawn by donkeys brought home orange ears of corn, boxes of apples, and brushwood collected in the forest for kindling. Bonfires were lit on the border strips, producing gray smoke that crept over the earth and dispersed on the riverbank.

Toward evening, the weary villagers would come back to their homes, and before going to bed they would sit outside on the wooden benches that propped up the fences, to have a chat with the neighbors, exchange news, or simply enjoy some company.

Gradually, the valley would start to prepare for the winter, taking its time, to be sure nothing was forgotten. Lara associated this season with a festive mood, with the holiday and the preparations for it, in which she loved to take part, helping her mother.

Once winter had locked up the valley, the residents, with nothing else to do, would kill time by paying one another visits, gathering around the table of an evening to drink wine as they sang old songs, reminisced, and told the ancient legends. Lara's brothers were especially fond of tales about the bandit Jokolo, famous throughout the Caucasus.

"Do you know the story of Jokolo?" said Lara, suddenly brightening as she cast me a sidelong, inquiring look. "At home, everyone knows it."

I said I didn't, and she smiled, as if happy to tell the story to someone who'd never heard it before.

"Our village is named for him, but now I think we got more from him than just his name. . . . It's as if his fate were tied to the place and were just waiting to strike, then take possession of the people and change them. Just as it changed my children. After all this, I really don't know if it's a good thing or a bad one."

She paused, then began again in a very different tone, as if reciting from memory: "Above all, Jokolo loved his freedom—he refused to observe any rules that limited him, or bow down to any king or shah, however powerful. He formed a band of cutthroats and outlaws like him, and as their chief, he lived a wild life in the mountains, robbing the rich, the governors and tax collectors. He never harmed the poor, because what would there be to steal from them? He preferred them to help him, whether out of gratitude or fear, by hiding him from the police, warning him of danger, or sending their sons to join his insurgents, and not refusing him shelter or assistance in time of need. And that's how it was—the poor villagers from the Caucasian gorges admired him; many saw him as their heroic defender. The word used in the Caucasus to describe such men is *abrek*, which means both 'outcast' and 'avenger.' Almost without exception, the boys from the highland *auls* dreamed of growing up to be famous bandits like Selim Khan or Jokolo, or at least of joining a robber band. But even a daredevil like Jokolo was bound to come to grief one day. For many years, he eluded his pursuers—until, at last, some soldiers tracked him down in the Pankisi Gorge and surrounded the farm where he was hiding. Jokolo had fallen into a trap. He realized that he and his handful of men had no chance of winning a fight against the soldiers, who outnumbered them several times over and were better armed. He knew that this time he couldn't break free of the siege, but he didn't want to die, either—life was still dear to him. So, he chose to negotiate with the Kakhetian princes, and after some lengthy bargaining, he finally accepted their terms. He agreed to lay down his weapons and disband his men, and also to give back the stolen treasure he hadn't yet distributed. He renounced banditry and swore to live in peace with the Kakhetian princes. They agreed that he and his fellow outlaws could choose a place for themselves in the Pankisi Gorge, build houses there, and start a new life. The *abreks* chose a site on the Alazani River, and from then on the village was called by the name of their leader, 'Jokolo.'"

But instead of the stories about bandits, Lara preferred the legend about some shepherds from the northern side of the Caucasus who, while searching the mountains for stray sheep, lost their own way in the dense, unfamiliar forest. They wandered across to the Georgian side, all the way to the gorge along the Alazani River, where they stopped for the night. The next morning, they were so delighted by the place where they'd chosen to break their journey that they decided to stay there forever. Making this decision was easy because they'd instantly found a source of freshwater, which had sprung up in the night at the spot where they'd stuck the staffs they'd leaned on while crossing the mountains. Then, to their amazement, they noticed that some swallows were weaving a nest on the staffs. They saw these as clear signs that they couldn't possibly ignore.

Lara liked the legend of the lost sheep because it confirmed everything she believed in, and it offered the promise of everything she desired. The gorge was her home and her destiny, she was meant to live here, and this was where all her dreams would come true. Nothing had to be changed or pushed forward. She only had to let matters take their course for her destiny to come true—what was meant to happen would happen.

No wonder she couldn't wait for the winter evenings. Eager to hear the fables and singing, she prayed for them to last as long as possible and for nothing to disturb them. She felt that as long as those peaceful winter evenings continued, she had all she needed to be happy. And so did everyone else in the gorge, which, from a small scrap of earth tucked in among the mountains, had become a self-contained, separate world.

Even when she grew up to be a serious young woman old enough to marry, she never thought of the Pankisi Gorge as a parochial backwater that restricted her movements and thoughts, the sort of place a person should escape as soon as possible. Aware of what had happened to others, each of its inhabitants knew roughly what lay in store for them—how their fortunes would turn out, what they could count on, and what was best ignored without wasting any time.

The constancy of life in the Pankisi Gorge gave its people a sense of certainty and security. So they guarded it like precious treasure, like something extremely sacred. Every deviation from the set, familiar ways, every tiny change was recorded in memory as an unusual event. But it was seen as a worry that disturbed the peace and introduced unnecessary confusion rather than as a pleasant change to the tedious monotony.

Two such events were fixed in Lara's memory. The first was the visit of a famous actor, who came to her school to recite poems by the Georgian poet Vazha-Pshavela.

Lara already knew about Vazha-Pshavela because they'd studied him in school. She was surprised he had abandoned a wealthy, sophisticated life—first in Telavi and then Tbilisi and, later, in faraway Moscow—to return to his village and live like a simple peasant. Along with his old life, he had dropped his family name and adopted the name of the province where he lived. His contemporaries thought he was eccentric, but they loved his poetry, and when he died, all Georgia was plunged into mourning.

The story of the poet's life merely reinforced Lara's conviction that the Pankisi Gorge was her proper place, and her love of it was intensified by his poems, which were full of his love of nature and his admiration for the people of the Caucasus valleys.

Before beginning his recital in the school assembly hall, the famous actor had solemnly announced that he envied everyone in the room because they could consider themselves compatriots or neighbors of the great poet. But while he was declaiming the poems, the children who'd been made to sit in the front row as a punishment began to giggle as he sprayed saliva, pulled faces, and rolled his eyes to adopt an inspired pose. The furious actor insisted that the little brats be expelled from the room, or else he'd have to stop the performance. But Lara listened to the poetry as if spellbound, unable to believe that the village where Vazha-Pshavela had lived was so close to her own valley.

The actor's performance at her school was Lara's first experience of the compelling power of art. She felt as if her soul had taken wing. She couldn't tear her eyes away from the artist as he declaimed the poems, especially the ones she knew by heart. Speechless with delight, she silently moved her lips, repeating the words after him. She'd never imagined poems from the school textbook could be turned into music, brought to life, and acted out through the voice, face, and gestures. The strong emotion she felt soon brought on a desire to take part in this sort of mystery herself, by performing onstage.

Not long after the actor's visit, an old friend of her father's came to visit. He had left the gorge many years earlier to live on the other side of the mountains. Summoned back to Pankisi by telegram to attend his cousin's funeral, he was taking the opportunity to look up his old friends, including Lara's father.

He talked about Grozny, the prosperous big city where he lived, and how different his life was there from the one he'd had here in the gorge. He said he sometimes missed it, but only in the way we miss times that are past and gone, our youth that will never return. But he'd never swap his life in the Chechen city for his old life in the gorge.

"Everything's bigger and faster there, and there's more of it," he said. "But you probably don't have much to worry about here, do you?"

He said that in Grozny the houses were as large as the mountains here, and the streets were as wide as the gorges. People even drove their cars along them at night, when they were lit up until dawn by streetlights and lamps in the windows of the houses. If they wished, the women could go out to work, just like the men.

"We have large houses too. In Tbilisi. I've seen them!" exclaimed Lara, who'd been listening to the adults' conversation. She'd been on a school outing to the Georgian capital, the first time she'd ever left the gorge. "And theaters!"

But then she stopped short, terrified, because among the Kists, it was unacceptable for children, especially girls, to speak in the presence of adults without being spoken to. Her father glared at her sternly, but his guest just smiled and stroked her cheek with a rough hand.

"Compared with my city, Tbilisi is like a wooden fort compared with a palace," he said. "We have a theater too, and what a grand one! More than one. You can go to the theater every night of the week in Grozny."

Lara never forgot this conversation, and she grew curious about the city where the theaters were open every night—and where the Chechens lived, the Kists' ancestral race.

But she still believed in the self-sufficiency and separate identity of the Pankisi Gorge as a place on the sidelines, far from the world and its problems, joys, and worries—far from everything lying beyond it.

The Pankisi Gorge officially starts just past the boundaries of Akhmeta, a small town with public offices and courts, to which the villages in the gorge are legally subordinate. But perhaps the real gateway to Pankisi is farther on, past almost all the villages, and the copses, meadows, and fallow land that lie beyond them, at the point where the gorge narrows and imperceptibly comes closer to the road. Here we find Duisi, the largest of all the villages in the gorge and the only one to have a local bazaar, a hospital, a cultural center, two mosques, and, above all, the last police station in the region.

"Duisi is at the narrowest point in the gorge. Beyond it, the villages follow on from one another." When Lara talked about the gorge, her face relaxed and the weariness left it. "On the western riverbank, you'd be in Jokolo before you knew it; one step more, and you'd be in Birkiani; then finally in Jibakhevi. On the eastern bank, across the bridge, you'll find Upper, Middle, and Lower Khalatsani; then Dumasturi and then Omalo, from where you can follow the passes all the way to Tusheti. And over the mountains to the west lies the Tianeti Gorge, where the Khevsurians live."

As a child, like every little girl, whether living under the North Star or the Southern Cross, Lara dreamed of being a princess, like in a fairy tale. That's what the neighbors and her mother's friends called her, anyway. They were charmed by her beauty, her regular features, her eyes, and hair the color of ripe chestnuts. They predicted a successful life for her, with a good husband—she was sure to make her parents proud and bring them joy.

Lara's other great dream, though she had kept it to herself, was a genuine desire to perform on the stage—to act in plays, to dance, and to sing the many songs she knew.

While telling me these facts at the McDonald's in Tbilisi, she had a smile on her face, as if embarrassed to talk about her childhood dream. Although she had passionately wanted it to come true, she had realized it probably never would. She had promised herself that even so, she wouldn't feel disappointed and wouldn't regard her life as a failure. Anyway, she couldn't understand how anyone could be dissatisfied or embittered about life, even if it hadn't turned out exactly as they'd hoped.

"We have to make the most of life, but we have to look after it too," she said.

And what are our dreams for?

"Our dreams aren't meant to come true, because as soon as they do, they're over," she replied. "The point of our dreams is to make sure we never stop wanting to live. To remind us of that."

For many years, nothing occurred to suggest that Lara's life would ever go off course like a river stirred by spring storms and avalanches coming down from the mountains. On the contrary, every event, whether major or minor, made her life fuller and better, seeming to promise that her wishes would come true and that good and joyful times would be followed by even happier ones.

Much later, when she let herself reminisce, she sometimes found it hard to believe those days had gone by at such high speed. Yet she could remember every incident, every word, thought, impression, and feeling, as if it were yesterday.

Once she had graduated from high school in Pankisi, her parents let her go on studying. Their attitude was unusual. Generally, the teenage girls in the valley were destined to marry and have children rather than go to college.

Encouraged by Lara's teachers, who couldn't stop praising her talent, diligence, and desire to study, her parents acquiesced. They knew her, and they knew she wouldn't bring shame on them, she wouldn't forget herself, and above all, she wouldn't change; once she'd had a good look at the world, she'd come home to the valley and the old life mapped out for her by the current of the Alazani River.

Lara applied to the teaching institute in nearby Telavi, to be close to home, in case of need. There was no arts faculty at the Kakhetian academy, and it didn't train actors, singers, musicians, or dancers—only teachers. But Lara had no complaints.

She could see herself as a schoolteacher, giving lessons, writing on the board, explaining the complexities of algebra to the children gazing at her, revealing the secrets of nature to them, and teaching them to learn poems by heart. She felt she would enjoy this profession and that it wouldn't be very different from performing onstage or singing at a concert. And her reward would be the same sort of admiration and applause, the same gratitude from an audience, and the same satisfaction from doing a good job well. But she never finished her studies; she never defended her diploma or became a teacher, either.

"For family reasons," she said curtly, when I asked why she had dropped her studies.

This was clearly something she didn't want to talk about, and her adamant resistance made me think it must have had something to do with her emotions—in the Caucasus, that's a taboo subject.

The men will raise a toast at table to the love of their mothers, or to eternal brotherhood and friendship. They'll gush about their own sensitivity, fall into one another's arms and weep unashamedly when the conversation turns to their beloved homeland. But they won't show their children affection, ascribing their emotional restraint to parental concern and the need to prepare them for life, which is often harsh. And the children treat their fathers with respect rather than tenderness, as if showing the latter would reflect badly on their elders. If asked about their love for a woman, they shrug off the question or turn away, pretending not to hear. To them, showing your feelings, or even talking about them, is something indecent that diminishes the actual emotion.

Taught to be restrained by the men, the Caucasian women are also reluctant to talk about love in the presence of strangers. Lara wouldn't even tell me her husband's first name.

She had married him while she was training to be a teacher in Telavi. They had met in Jokolo during the summer vacation. He was from a family that used to live in the Pankisi Gorge but had moved to the other side of the mountains many years ago. He had come to visit some distant relatives and, also on business, to pay the locals an advance for the chestnuts they were going to pick for him in the fall.

Despite his family origins, he had been born in Chechnya and regarded himself as a Chechen. He was the first Chechen Lara had ever set eyes on. And he lived in Grozny, the city where the theaters were open every night.

They were instantly attracted to each other. But was it love?

"Curiosity, for sure. Or infatuation! He was like someone from another world, one I didn't know but was curious about. And he was a Chechen!" Lara was uncomfortable talking about it. "But love? It happens so rarely. Where I come from there's more of it in poems and romantic novels than in real life. But of course, we think about it, we daydream like everyone. But we don't expect it, and if it doesn't come along, we just get on with life."

Lara's parents didn't refuse him when he asked for her hand. And she accepted the proposal without much thought, figuring there was nothing to wait for. She didn't want to oppose the will of her elders, and here it was the parents, guided by their experience of life and their wisdom, who made the decisions about love and marriage for their sons and daughters.

In Caucasian villages, you could ask for a girl's hand or you could abduct her from her family home and then pray for her father and brothers to come around to the idea, which was how it usually ended. If, in the first surge of anger, the girl's family did not immediately swear to take violent revenge on the abductor and all his relatives, sooner or later they let themselves be placated, and eventually they gave the young couple their blessing. For what other choice was there but revenge, which could lead to multiple deaths and could last for generations? Even if they managed to rescue the girl from the kidnapper, who would want her as a wife, knowing she'd been another man's captive?

The Kists' world was shaped by a sacred, inviolable duty to observe their ancient, traditional laws and customs. It gave their lives direction, helped them make crucial choices, and dispelled their doubts. Yet it didn't leave them much liberty— especially in matters of love.

The young men were given more freedom than the young women; they could choose wives for themselves, including outsiders from neighboring valleys and even foreigners. Once married, those women became part of their husbands' families, were taught the rules of their new life, and became just like their female neighbors; from the day they were born, their children were regarded as local.

Girls from the valley had no such privileges. No father would have let his daughter marry an outsider; nor would he have accepted a foreigner into his family. He'd have forbidden her to see him, and in the worst instance, he'd have arranged for her to be abducted by one of the local young men and then given his blessing to *their* marriage. The young woman's protests, laments, and threats that she'd rather take her own life than spend it with someone she didn't love would be in vain. Lara knew a girl who'd been married against her will, but a few days after the wedding, when she ran away from her new home and back to her parents, her father told her to get out. Her mother wrung her hands and begged her to return to her husband, not to bring shame on the family and not to make them a laughingstock. The accepted view was that, with time, every pain diminished and then vanished into oblivion, taking its original cause with it. Those were the rules, and they couldn't be changed if their world was going to survive.

For Lara, getting married meant saying goodbye not just to her family home, but to the entire valley, and moving across the mountains to live with her husband in Chechnya. She knew what to expect. The girls in the valley always moved in with their husbands straight after their wedding and became part of their families, breaking almost all ties with their own parental homes.

However, Lara's husband didn't rush her and even agreed that she could stay in Telavi to finish her studies, get her teacher's diploma, and only then come to live with him in Grozny. But his health declined—at least, that's what Lara said—and he sent for her without waiting for her to finish her course.

Her new home was a small apartment that, with help from her husband's family, they rented in downtown Grozny, not far from the Sunzha River. It was on the tenth floor in one of the large, bright buildings that surrounded a small, round space known to the locals as Minutka, meaning "minute," because it served as a transit point for bus and taxi passengers who stopped here for a minute or so to change their mode of transport. Lara had never imagined you could live so high above the ground, nor had she ever seen such large buildings before, housing so many people at once.

At first, the huge size of the city made her head spin, and so did the pace of life—fast, furious, and impatient. Even late at night she could hear noise from the street below through the closed windows of her sky-high apartment—car horns, intermittent voices, and the shouts of drivers and people selling things at the nearby market.

At first, whenever she went outside, she felt lost and alien, but she soon got used to her new location. As the days went by, gradually she stopped feeling the sense of exclusion and the threat that had come with every walk she took. Soon she wasn't afraid of life in the big city.

Instead, Grozny began to amaze and delight her more and more. Its wealth and splendor were a treat, as were the comforts and the seemingly unlimited opportunities it offered. Lara had never known such liberty before. Life in the city meant breaking free from the old customs and code of conduct she used to regard as sacred and immutable. Lara had no intention of denying or forgetting them, but little by little, her old life in the valley was becoming like a photograph that fades with age, just an important memory. Now the big city was her home, and she felt a growing certainty that this was her proper place on earth.

She realized she was becoming more tied to it, gradually putting down deeper roots. Taking part in the life of the city gave her just as much joy as she'd felt in the sunny Pankisi Gorge, where the twinkling waters of the Alazani River had delighted her. Now she saw the splendors of Grozny as her own.

She felt a surge of strength and pride at the sight of the wide, busy streets full of cars and people. She was thrilled by the rich, multistory houses in the city center, the factories in the suburbs that gave people jobs and an income, and the stores where you could choose the goods from the shelves, including items she'd never seen before. She admired the parks, schools, cinemas, and especially the theaters, which still stirred her imagination. Her old dreams were returning, but without any of the dull pain that comes with a sense of loss.

Compared with the gorge, where the heat of summer brought life to a standstill, the whirling world of the big city made her feel as if any plan could be realized, however wild or long abandoned. Here anything could happen, any wish could come true—you could even turn back time.

A factor that made it easier for Lara to leave the valley and get used to the city was that the people here spoke Chechen. She knew the Kists regarded themselves as descendants of the Chechens, but once in the city, she was amazed to hear her own language on the radio. She couldn't understand every single word and occasionally lost track of what was being said. Thrilled and surprised, she stared at the speaker as it poured out words and phrases that the Kists used every day. She was overjoyed to find that the Kist dialect was essentially the same as the Chechen language, and that the Chechens really were their brothers, separated only by the mountains. So their capital, Grozny, was her city too, and its wealth and greatness, this entire wonderful world, belonged to her too, because they'd been created by Chechens.

As an inhabitant of the Pankisi Gorge, Lara hadn't expected more from fate than the typical local fortunes. But since moving to the city, she had become more acquisitive, wanting more, not just materially, but also personally.

At the time, if anyone had asked her if these were the best days of her life, she might have been quite put out. She'd have said she was only just starting to make the best of life and that so far her experiences in the city were limited—the truly wonderful, very best times were yet to come. But years later, she'd have agreed that those days in Grozny, at the start of her adult life, were in fact the happiest. If only she had known that, perhaps she'd have been able to enjoy them more, without impatiently looking out for what was yet to come.

Everything seemed to be heading in the right direction. Her husband took care of her and of their home, and Lara bore him two strong, healthy sons, first Shamil and then, three years later, Rashid. She had fulfilled her husband's dream, the greatest dream of every man in the Caucasus, for whom fathering a son is the confirmation of his own value. In a flood of gratitude and affection, her husband promised that as soon as the children were old enough, if she was still very keen, Lara could go back to school.

When Rashid reached the age of three and could go to pre-school, Lara enrolled at the drama school in Grozny, which was famous throughout the Caucasus. Now her life would acquire special meaning.

At first it was like a dream. She felt light and confident, as in spring. She felt as if she weren't walking, but floating along the city streets. Each morning, she'd see her sons off to school and her husband to the factory, then she'd race to the academy at top speed to study stage performance, the magical art of por-traying another person, of thinking and feeling like them, and sharing their troubles and choices.

In a different situation, this skill might have been an escape from an unsuccessful life, a way of creating at will the illusion of being someone else. But Lara had everything she wanted and never felt the need to become another person.

"It was like being in a movie. It was all so perfect that it couldn't have been better," she said. "The city, the houses, the parks, the factories, the streets, and the limousines gliding by. Apparently there were more expensive cars on the streets of Grozny than anywhere else in the Caucasus. Life was beautiful, and we thought we were too."

Before she knew it, two years had gone by. Nor did she notice when things began to take a turn for the worse. She couldn't pinpoint the moment that spoiled her carefree mood, bringing the first doubts and anxiety, cold and heavy like a stone—and the feeling that something was going wrong.

Busy with her own world, moving between her home and the theater, she didn't need to think about anything else. One day after supper, when her sons had gone to bed, she was ironing some new curtains when she happened to hear the TV news. Her husband was on the couch drinking a mug of tea and watching television.

"These curtains weren't expensive, but apparently they're Italian. There were blue ones too, but beige goes better with the living room. Maybe I should get the other ones for the boys' room? The ones in there are very old. And they could do with bigger beds—they'll soon grow out of the ones they have."

Both boys were big, especially Rashid. They grew faster than all their peers. Lara was pleased when her friends nodded their heads in appreciation at the sight of them. "They're going to be very big and strong," they'd say admiringly. "The sort of men that do well in life."

"And we could think about some new furniture in general."

Without answering, her husband went on staring at the television screen. The factory where he worked was closed because the orders had stopped coming in from Moscow, and soon after that the money to pay the wages had dried up too. He had lost his job, but he was sure there was nothing to worry about. Sooner or later they'd open the factory again—it couldn't possibly be left idle for long. In the meantime, he and a friend were going to start up a stall at the market, where they'd earn more than in the public sector. And they were also considering a business venture that, if it took off, would bring in more income than his annual salary at the factory.

Plenty of people in Grozny lived off private enterprise. They had left their public-sector jobs to open stores, workshops, and small manufacturing plants. But mainly, they traded. They were always traveling to other places, where they bought goods cheaply and then sold them at a higher price at home. And although there was an increasing number of these companies, the city wasn't getting any poorer. On the contrary, life there seemed ever more energetic and stylish.

Lara quite often heard old people in the city expressing their concerns that the Chechens' wealth, the local deposits of crude oil, all their excitement, and their inflated view of themselves had antagonized the Russians, who would do everything they could to take it away from them. "It'd be different if we were an independent country, like Georgia, Armenia, or Azerbaijan," they were saying. "Then Russia couldn't do anything to us."

Lara took it as nothing but idle gossip, which was never in short supply in the Caucasus. But that evening, as she was encouraging her husband to buy some new furniture, she heard something on TV that sowed the first seeds of anxiety in her.

". . . taking advantage of temporary difficulties . . . political troublemakers and common criminals . . . cannot be permitted any longer . . . to penalize and restore order . . . to put a stop . . . at any price . . ."

"Are they talking about us?" asked Lara, surprised to recognize the streets of downtown Grozny on the screen.

"And how!" retorted her husband. "Who else?"

"Is it serious?"

"It's just hot air. They're just trying to scare us. There's nothing to get upset about."

Lara gave no answer. But she didn't buy the curtains for the boys' room. Or the new beds. Or any other new furniture. She was never going to buy any new furniture again.

She felt as if there were something blocking her; she couldn't escape the insistent thought that now was not the right time, she must wait. A strange feeling kept popping up like a bad dream, just for an instant, sometimes a little longer, before vanishing. But it always left a mark, a choking sensation in her throat. By now she couldn't hold back her tears, and her sense of sorrow stifled any desire to take action and made every good idea seem pointless.

At this stage, she didn't feel threatened, but simply lost her solid faith in the idea that life was good and that as long as she did her best, nothing could go wrong. She finally realized how little depended on her when, one fine September afternoon, she'd finished work at the theater and was on her way home with her sons.

First she'd gone to fetch Shamil from school, and then together they'd picked up Rashid from kindergarten. They headed home on foot, through the city. On bright afternoons like this one, flooded with summer sunshine and warmth, it was a sin to travel in a crowded bus amid the exhaust fumes.

She let the boys go ahead. They walked along, engrossed in conversation, waving their arms and the ice creams she'd bought for them from a street vendor. Though three years younger, Rashid was almost as tall as Shamil. Despite the difference in age, they'd always been very close, like twins. Rashid thought the world of his older brother, and Shamil kept Rashid from harm.

When they reached the main square, she called to them to stop. Ignoring their protests, she grabbed each boy by the hand.

Outside the presidential palace, one of the tallest and grandest buildings in the city, there was a huge crowd of people. Lara remembered that someone at the theater had mentioned that this afternoon there was going to be a rally at which the president would speak in person.

She knew him from the television news, which she now watched every day. The president wore a military uniform and a large officer's hat, which he sometimes swapped for a flight cap. No wonder—he was a military man, a bomber pilot, and in the Soviet air forces he had risen to the rank of general.

At first the Russians had regarded him as their man, someone who would guarantee them peace and quiet in the Caucasus. But then he started inciting the Chechens to copy the Georgians and demand their own separate state, independent of Russia, after which they had elected him as their president. Now he was seen in Moscow as a traitor. On Russian TV, they were calling him "a dangerous troublemaker," "the dictator of a banana republic," and "the Godfather," saying he'd bring misfortune on his nation and that innocent people would have to pay for his rampant ambitions. But his compatriots admired him—more than that, they worshipped him like a saint. No other Chechen had risen to such heights, and his people were proud of him. He had won their hearts when, instead of living in comfort and prosperity in Moscow or Saint Petersburg, he had turned his back on an easy life and returned to the Caucasus to be their leader. Whenever he was due to appear at a rally, the whole city came to hear him speak.

He was making his speech when Lara and her sons entered the square in front of the palace. So many people had gathered there that the police had stopped the traffic in the neighboring streets. Lara couldn't see the dais from which the president was speaking, but his voice echoed far and wide through loud-speakers suspended from the trees and lampposts.

"We are not Russia's enemies, but we're not going to be its slaves anymore, either. We are free people, and we have the right to determine our own fate, to decide what we want and what we don't want."

After each of the president's declarations, the crowd burst into loud cheers and shouted his name. There were even cries of *Allahu akbar!* "God is great!"

"We must decide for ourselves. Would we rather live like servants, on our knees, endlessly kowtowing? Or would we rather die for the Chechens to live like free people, with our heads held high and our clenched fists proudly raised to strike?"

"Long live the president! Hurray! *Allahu akbar!*" came the crowd's ardent response.

"So what are we going to do when they come here with guns and tanks? Let our heads droop and surrender? Or would you rather defend our liberty, even at the price of war? Even at the price of death? Slavery or liberty—make your choice!"

"Liberty! War! We want to fight, we want to fight!" roared the crowd.

That evening after supper, Lara once again asked her husband what was going to happen and if there was still nothing to fear. Perhaps it'd be better, safer, to leave the city and go to Pankisi, to her parents' house, for instance?

"To Georgia?" said her husband in amazement.

All the unsettling events on the television news that seemed to be getting closer, making her want to run away, had already been happening in Georgia for ages: they'd had one war after another, each worse than the last. There were bearded men with rifles in the streets, shooting; fires, refugees, and homeless people; and the trees and houses along Rustaveli Avenue, Tbilisi's main road, were scarred by exploding shells. There was also exhausting uncertainty, helplessness, no electricity, endless darkness and extreme cold, empty stores and people stuck outside them waiting for God knows what, unable to cope with their misfortune, not knowing where to seek help or where to turn to complain.

She had seen it for herself in Tbilisi, where she'd been once in recent years, to find a doctor for her ailing father. Their neighbors in Pankisi had advised her against the journey, warning her that there was fighting and that in such unsettled times it was better not to leave home. She had ignored them, figuring they were being overcautious and that their stories about war were exaggerated. But when she arrived, she was horrified, and she had never forgotten what she saw there. She thanked God that she had moved across the mountains to Grozny.

"Do you really think it's a good idea to go to Georgia?" said her husband. She thought she could hear derision in his voice, with an undertone of animosity.

She didn't answer, but yes, she did think so. She'd leave for Georgia this very minute if she could. And it wasn't Georgia she wanted to go to, but home.

Gradually her anxiety pushed out every other thought and emotion. It wouldn't let her focus on anything else. Neither her domestic duties nor her rehearsals at the theater could distract her; suddenly they had paled and become pointless.

She had never known an emotion as painful as the crippling fear she felt for her children. Perhaps that was why it affected her so badly. It was nonstop fear, day and night, that kept telling her to get away from Grozny, as fast and as far as possible. She knew that sooner or later she was going do it, regardless of anyone or anything else—including her husband, who couldn't perceive the danger and who refused to accept that there were clouds gathering over the city. Whenever she mentioned it, he lost patience. And Lara was upset with herself for waiting for his consent, for losing time, for toying with fate.

"Georgia," he'd say disdainfully, "what a bunch of clowns on horseback . . ."

He'd say the theater had muddled her wits; she'd read too much, seen too much nonsense, but real life was not a stage show.

"So now what? Are you really willing to lose your role?" he asked. Toward the end of the year, they were putting on a new play at the theater, and Lara had been cast in one of the leading female parts. She had never played such a major role before, and she was greatly looking forward to opening night. "Won't you regret it?"

To her own surprise, she felt no regret at the thought that she might not act in the show. She felt increasingly trapped in the city and just wanted to leave it as fast as possible.

"Please, let's get out of here," she begged.

She wanted to go home to the gorge, where her mother and father lived. The mere thought of it restored her sense of security and certainty about the future. Nothing had changed there since she had left. Most of Georgia had suffered turmoil, but in the remote Pankisi Gorge, life had remained quiet and peaceful. Everything was still the same as before.

So despite the war that was raging in Georgia, the gorge was a safe place. She knew this because, once a year, she went to visit her parents and her old home. She always took the children with her, rather than burdening her husband with the need to care for them in her absence. Even so, he could have refused to let her make those journeys, and she was grateful to him for never having objected.

In the Caucasus, a married woman did not maintain her ties with her old family. If Lara and her husband had lived in the gorge, among the Kists, or in one of the Chechen *auls*, they would have had to follow this rule. But in the big city founded by the Russians and where Russians made up half the population, the customs were more relaxed.

"Let's get out of here," she begged her husband in the fall, when icy rain had started falling, filling the air with piercing cold and turning the ground into viscous, slippery mud.

But he still wouldn't hear of leaving the city and moving to the gorge. With a reckless stubbornness that Lara couldn't understand, he refused to move, as if leaving meant failure, rather than salvation.

"You want to abandon all this?" he'd say.

"But what do we have here? What's keeping us?" She was surprised he couldn't see what she could see. "We can start all over again, and we'll soon have everything we have now."

"But why? What are you so afraid of? War?"

She said yes.

"War? Here?"

"It broke out . . . in Georgia . . ."

"Georgia!" he snapped. "This isn't Georgia."

By late fall, the tension in the city was almost palpable. In the streets, there were more and more people carrying rifles, not just men in uniform, but ordinary civilians too. The conversations at kitchen tables, at work, and in the stores were increasingly often about war, and so was the TV news broadcast from Moscow.

People began to disappear. More and more of them were seen in their courtyards and driveways cramming suitcases, bags, and bundles into their cars; anything that didn't fit inside was carefully stacked on the roof. They never said where they were going or when they'd be back, nor did they say goodbye to anyone. They just checked that they'd packed everything and made sure the cords securing the luggage were tied tightly. Then they drove off without looking back.

At the theater, the shows were canceled. The managers announced that rehearsals were indefinitely suspended too, so the actors needn't come to work and wouldn't be paid for the unexpected days off.

Lara also noticed that people were buying more food. At first she thought it was just her imagination, but soon she was buying more than usual too, more than they actually needed. Like others, she bought sugar, jam, salt, canned food, oil, and laundry detergent, more than she could fit in the kitchen cupboards or on the shelves in the pantry. It annoyed her husband, who complained that she was wasting money, which was running low, especially now that the theater had closed and they had no idea when, if ever, Lara would go back to work.

She realized that everything that went against his judgment of the present and future situation annoyed him. His firm belief that he was right gave him a sense of security and perhaps a sense of his own worth too. Lara thought he was losing his bearings, yet he continued to insist on taking no action. He simply couldn't or wouldn't see the threat, and he regarded Lara's increasingly persistent pleas to leave the city as a betrayal. He was beginning to see her as an enemy. They were drifting apart, though she still believed they'd weather it—this was just the kind of temporary crisis that affects every marriage. But her fears for their relationship had to take second place to the responsibility she felt toward the children. She had to get them out of the city at any cost; she had to protect them from danger. Whenever she saw them playing war games in the yard, her determination became stronger. The boys had always played soldiers and often made the sandbox into a battlefield, but now they never seemed to play any other game.

One day at about noon, some soldiers drove into their courtyard in two cars. Lara didn't know the name of the middle-aged man in charge of them, but she had seen him in the neighborhood before. As she watched him commanding the soldiers, she realized that lately she'd seen him more often.

He stood by one of the cars, smoking a cigarette as he waited for his men to summon everyone from the apartment blocks surrounding the courtyard. The soldiers were young and unshaven. They wore military uniforms from the Russian barracks that had been occupied by the president's men some time ago. That incident had been reported on the television news. Lara couldn't understand why the Russians, who were happy to heap abuse on the Chechen president and had threatened to deprive him of power, had left the city without firing a single shot, abandoning their barracks full of weapons, ammunition, uniforms, and other military equipment. Straight after that, army vehicles had become a common sight in the city, driven by bearded soldiers like the ones who had appeared outside Lara's home.

Plenty of people had come down into the yard by now. In those days, very few of them were working. Instead they sat at home, waiting to see what would happen. The commander crushed his cigarette underfoot, cleared his throat, and said he had come on the president's orders, as leader of the local civil militia, which had been formed in case of war.

"It probably won't come to anything, but as we all know, better safe than sorry," he said. "Better to know in advance what to do if anything happens than to be asking questions later, once it's too late."

He explained that the president had ruled that all the civil militia commanders should meet with the people, introduce themselves, and show their faces, so that in case of need, the population would know who could help them with problems, questions, or anything at all—if a stranger or anyone suspicious appeared in their neighborhood, for instance, they should immediately come and report it to him.

He said the most important thing was to start getting the basements ready to be shelters. Just in case, because it was unlikely that the Russians would decide to attack the city. They probably wouldn't, they'd step back, and the president would find a way to come to terms with them. But if it ever came to a period of fighting, and especially aerial bombardment, the people must have somewhere to hide. So they should haul some mattresses, cabinets, furniture, and blankets down into the basement. As winter was approaching, it would be a good idea to stock the basements with stoves and firewood. But be sure to position things so that they didn't block the passages, doors, or windows.

He told them to stock up on water, food, oil lamps, candles, matches, and cigarettes.

"Just in case," he stressed again. "If nothing happens, those items will be useful at home anyway. Am I making sense?"

Lara so badly wanted to believe him! If only it would work out as he said.

"And no vodka!" he warned. "If something does happen and someone gets it into his head to drink, he'll bitterly regret it!"

Finally he asked the people if they understood everything and if they had any more questions for him.

"So is there going to be a war or not?" someone from the back said.

"How should I know?" he replied. "What will be, will be, but I wish it would just start. All this waiting for God knows what is driving everyone up the wall."

The next day, Lara refused to wait any longer, or to ask her husband's permission. She told him she was taking the boys out of the city, to the countryside—they weren't going very far, just to Ingushetia, not across into Georgia or all the way to the Pankisi Gorge. And only for a few days, until everything calmed down and the situation was clearer. They'd sit out the worst of it and then come home. Her husband didn't reply, but he plainly wasn't going with them. "Do as you wish," he muttered at last, and for the first time in ages, Lara felt relief and tranquility. Now she knew that whatever happened, she'd survive, and she'd be able to keep her children from harm.

At first light, she was ready in the hall with two suitcases and a backpack. She told the boys to say goodbye to their father. He said he'd keep an eye on things and that when they got back he'd take the whole family to the movies and then to a café for cakes and ice cream. There he stood, leaning against the door frame with a solemn, slightly sulky look on his face as they went down the stairs to the courtyard. That was the last time Lara ever saw him.

The gorge was almost deserted—or so claimed Lara's brother, who had borrowed a car to come fetch them from the Ingush village of Karabulak, where, with thousands of other refugees from Grozny, they had stopped after leaving the city. On the way, he told her the news, including the fact that most of the Kists, especially the younger ones, had gone abroad to look for work and to get away from war and lawlessness in Georgia. *And a good thing too*, thought Lara as she gazed at the abandoned villages.

She glanced at Shamil and Rashid, in the backseat. Tired by the journey, they were staring out the car window. The older boy was nine now, the younger six. Both born in Grozny, they had been registered as Chechens. They spoke Chechen and knew Russian but not a word of Georgian. Now they were going to become Georgians, so they'd have to learn the language and live the Georgian way.

"It'll be hard for them to start again and to grow up without a father," said her brother at the wheel.

"They'll get used to it," she replied without hesitation. She figured that if there were fewer people in the villages now, it'd be easier for her sons to assimilate in their new home. They'd have felt lost if they'd had to cope within a large crowd of strangers from the very first day. "Everything in its own time. It's going to be okay."

"Why shouldn't it be?" her brother agreed.

They'd been driving since dawn. From Karabulak, they went past Beslan and Vladikavkaz, then crossed the mountains on the road known as the Military Highway, which runs through the Caucasus range from north to south. They had set off at dawn to get as far as Tbilisi by nightfall.

"It's only one hundred and twenty-five miles, but you drive and drive, and it's endless," complained her brother.

He had insisted on coming to fetch them, although Lara had said it was a waste of effort and she could get to Tbilisi by cab. The cab drivers took up to five passengers at a time, but Lara was ready to pay for five seats for herself and the boys to travel as a threesome. But her father and brothers refused to hear of it. They were adamant that in such a restless, wartime situation it was dangerous for her to travel on her own with the children.

Only one hundred and twenty-five miles, and it's like another world, Lara thought. First they spent ages climbing up switchbacks into the mountains. But once they had gone through the Jvari Pass and past Mount Kazbek, the highest peak in the region, and were finally going downhill, Lara felt that no power on earth could make her turn back now.

She knew she'd done the right thing by giving up the life she'd been leading until now, and she had no regrets. But she was glad she didn't have to give her sons an explanation for the choice she'd made for them, or tell them why their father hadn't come too, or when they'd be going home. They hadn't cried and didn't even seem perturbed, nor had they asked any questions. They just did as she told them. As usual—as she had taught them.

They had always been polite and obedient. She never had to say anything twice or argue with them about anything. They were closer to her than to their father. They were afraid of him, but they talked and joked with her, and came to her for advice and comfort. As children, they were hers. But as teenagers, they would pass from their mother's care to their father's, for him to teach them how to be men. "Everything's going to be all right," she consoled herself.

The road ran in a wide arc around South Ossetia, which for several years had been in the grip of war between the Georgians and the Ossetians. Dusk was falling when they reached Mtskheta, and by the time they arrived in Tbilisi it was completely dark. Her brother had decided they would stay the night here with a friend of his who lived close to the city center, on Chitaia Street, near the railroad station and the Dinamo soccer stadium.

Cold rain was falling, and the city had vanished in the dark. It looked as if the only lights in the streets were the dazzling car headlamps. Although the Georgian war had ended, there was still no electricity in Tbilisi, no heating, and nothing in the stores. On David Agmashenebeli Avenue, a patrol stopped them. The men didn't look like policemen, but they were carrying guns. Although it was dark, they said the car had bald tires, so Lara's brother would have to pay a fine. He tried to argue, but Lara took the money from her wallet and handed it to the patrol leader. Without writing out a fine, he told them to go, while his men stopped the next car.

The Chechen friend who put them up for the night had nothing to eat but tea and a few sugar lumps, which he handed out to the boys like candy. It was freezing cold in his apartment, but the electricity was rationed and could be switched on for only a few hours in the middle of the night, according to a schedule issued by the authorities. People made their plans for the day depending when it would be on. Some of them had to get up in the middle of the night to have a hot bath or do the laundry.

"It's impossible to live here," their host complained.

But Lara knew her own mind. Next day, they continued their journey through gray, impoverished Tbilisi to Kakheti and then homeward to the Pankisi Gorge. She couldn't have found a better or safer place anywhere on earth. Here, out of the way, the war would never reach them. Here she could hide away with her children, sitting out the bad times. She'd protect them from the sight of injustice, cruelty, and killing, and from the evil that comes out of people when they're forced to fight for survival—or when they feel they have power over the lives of others and can do whatever they want to them with impunity. Lara didn't want her sons to be exposed to all that in their youth, or for it to start seeming normal or ordinary to them. But in the gorge they'd be safe, and evil wouldn't have access to them.

They had passed Akhmeta and Matani, the last Georgian village before the gorge, when snow began to fall from the heavily clouded sky. At first the snowfall was very light, almost invisible. But suddenly it covered the moldy brown grass, the leafless bushes, and the gray, muddy earth, coating everything pure white.

"We'll be just in time for dinner," Lara's brother said.

Although she wasn't there at the time, Lara had a clear vision of her older son's death. It was a hot summer night, and the cloudless sky above Aleppo was bright with stars.

Shamil was on his way back from night combat, or from a meeting. He knew so many languages that he was always being summoned to translate for the insurgent commanders who had come to Syria from all over the world to fight in what they saw as a holy war. As devout Muslims—especially those who had only recently discovered the true faith—they wanted to play their part, as a special form of purification that would guarantee them salvation.

In Syria, Lara had been afraid of those clear nights when the government air force took advantage of the good visibility to carry out raids on the insurgent camps. She'd be abruptly woken by the dull echo of bombs exploding.

She had asked her son never to go out at those times, but to stay in his quarters in the suburbs of Aleppo. Somehow, she thought he'd be safer in the daytime than at night. While she was staying with him, he had remained indoors after dark, and when she left, he had promised to avoid nighttime outings, but she knew he wouldn't keep his word. He had been so eager for her to leave that he'd have said anything, made any promise at all just to be free of responsibility for her safety in a country in the grip of war.

So he was on his way back at night, from either combat or a meeting, in a large four-by-four. He was in the passenger seat, and his comrade, a volunteer from Chechnya, was driving. Or maybe Shamil was behind the steering wheel? He'd told her he liked driving; aimlessly roaming the back roads on his own helped him to relax and think things through. He'd said that at night the desert seemed to glow like a silver river in the moonlight, so brightly that you didn't have to switch on the headlamps.

It was one of those silver nights, and they must have been talking, to avoid falling asleep or to let out the emotions they'd built up during the fighting. They probably never heard the plane that was tracking them in the dark, or the sound of the missile it fired. But suddenly the missile exploded, engulfing their car in a ball of fire. They didn't suffer or feel fear, although Shamil wasn't killed on the spot.

His comrades dragged him from the wreckage severely wounded and immediately took him to the hospital across the Turkish border. He didn't regain consciousness, and as soon as they arrived, the doctors pronounced him dead.

They took his corpse back to Aleppo and buried him before dawn, in keeping with Muslim ritual, in a special tomb where only the *shahideen* were buried—the martyrs whose death in the holy war had earned them salvation and opened the gates of paradise. They declared him a hero and added his name to the list of the greatest martyrs. Lara saw a photograph of Shamil posted on a website in homage to those killed in action.

She had never imagined their belief in God would be so important and necessary to them, or that it was possible to have such strong faith. What if she'd known? But how could she have known?

No one in the Pankisi Gorge was as deeply religious as that. The Kists knew they were Muslims, but if any of them prayed at a Christian church rather than a mosque, it wasn't the end of the world. They were aware that life sometimes makes you do things in spite of yourself and that you need to be flexible in order to survive. "If you're forced to go pray at the Orthodox church, then go; it's just a building. If they make you wear a cross, then wear it; it's only a piece of metal. In your heart and soul, you'll still be a god-fearing Muslim." That's what they'd been taught a hundred years ago by Kunta-haji, the man whom the Kists and Chechens had regarded as their teacher and spiritual guide on earth.

Kunta-haji had also warned them against war, and called on his disciples to keep well away from it. "War is savagery. Do not believe that the Turkish sultan will liberate you. He's just as much of a satrap as the Russian tsar, and so are the Arab leaders, who shield their tyranny behind sharia, God's law. But God does not like war, and I implore you never to engage in it—unless enemies attack your farms, wanting to deprive you of your honor, faith, and identity. Then and only then should you rise up and fight to the last man. And let your weapons be your piety, wisdom, patience, honesty, and goodness. No enemy can overcome such strength. Sooner or later they'll have to yield and admit defeat. If you keep to the true path, no one will ever conquer you."

The Kists in the gorge honored the memory of Kunta-haji, calling themselves his disciples; some even went on pilgrimages to his mother Kheda's tomb on the Chechen side of the mountains (Kunta-haji was arrested on the tsar's orders and died in exile in Russia), and to a nearby sacred spring. But they didn't regard Kunta-haji's teachings as guidelines for how to live. To the people in the gorge, cut off from the outside world, he was a character from a folk legend. Passed down through the generations like the story of Jokolo the bandit and the other *abreks*, the tale of Kunta-haji reminded the Kists who they were, where they were from, and what distinguished them from others. To them, the Muslim faith was a characteristic, just as the Kyrgyz have slanted eyes or the Slavs have straw-colored hair. Saying "I am a Muslim" was not a declaration of faith, but a way of defining your place on the map, your preferences and customs. It wasn't a very spiritual statement at all.

Nor was faith, especially the Islamic kind, regarded as a source of pride. The Muslims were always the losers, beaten in every war by the Christians. For that reason alone, Islam was thought of as inferior, weaker, subordinate. It was something shameful and backward.

In fact, they regarded Christianity and all other religions as regressive too. The powers that had deposed the tsar and who now ruled Russia's entire empire claimed there was no god and that anyone who thought otherwise was rejecting modernity and progress. In other words, they were dangerous troublemakers who should be eradicated quickly and without mercy. The Soviet leaders scorned religious faith and those who refused to abandon it. "Who on earth, in the age of computers and space exploration, would believe in something that can't be proved?" they sneered. Religion is an anachronism—modern man is open-minded and cares about development, he can't possibly believe in God! And when mockery didn't help, they had the places of worship closed and the mullahs and priests thrown in jail or exiled to Siberia.

They insisted that life was not about denying pleasures and regarding them as nothing but sin. You only lived once—why mortify yourself in the hope of guaranteeing your posthumous salvation?

Though a child at the time, Lara could remember how on Sundays and other days the Christians regarded as sacred, people would come all the way from Tbilisi to hold special fêtes, with singing, dancing, *shashlik*, and vodka, carousels, shooting ranges, and raffles. Lara couldn't wait for those days to arrive.

When she was little, she used to go to the old mosque in Duisi with her mother. In the usual Muslim way, the men and women in the gorge prayed separately. Her mother used to take her on Fridays, when the *zikr* was performed in a special room.

Within the Islamic religion, *zikr* means intense praying with the aim of entering a trancelike state of spirituality that creates a sense of community with Allah. Most of the congregation did this in silent concentration, by saying prayers in their heart of hearts.

But in the gorge, the disciples of Kunta-haji, both men and women, usually praised God aloud, grouped together in a circle, by singing and shouting out all the divine names at the top of their voices. *La ilaha ill-Allah!* "There is no god greater than Allah!" They'd whirl about in euphoric prayer, which in the men's case often took the form of a menacing war dance.

This way of offering up prayers was a great favorite with the children in the gorge, and if Lara's husband had been living with them in Jokolo, he'd have taken his sons to the mosque to see the *zikr*, to watch the adults and learn the path to God and to salvation. But in Grozny, religion wasn't regarded as essential, and various daily responsibilities pushed it out of sight.

After moving to Grozny, Lara had neglected her faith, though she justified it to herself as normal practice there—this was city life, and there was no helping it. Most of the citizens probably wouldn't know where to find their local mosque and would regard the *zikr* as an outdated folk ritual. Or an old, abandoned custom, like the highland coats and sheepskin hats the men used to wear but that they now put on only for weddings and the ancient festivals still celebrated in the villages.

There was no such thing in the city, but in the Pankisi Gorge they were still a natural part of life. On returning to the gorge, Lara was ready to yield to its rules again and to drop her city habits. She also made that decision for her sons. They'd been born as Chechens, just as she had wanted; being members of the Chechen community was meant to secure them a better life. But now, for their own good, they were going to become Georgians, and in the first place, they'd be Georgian Chechens—that is, Kists. They were returning to her home, where no harm could come to them. There was no safer place for them.

Once she had settled in Jokolo again, Lara joined in with the duties assigned to members of the family and the community and adapted to the new pace of her life. She only had to remember the recent past and to watch and copy the others. She figured her sons would easily adapt too. Although their father wasn't with them, here they had their uncles, grandfather, stepbrothers, and various cousins at hand. Nobody was ever alone or left unsupported in the gorge.

Perhaps that was why she ignored her sons' dislike of the local school, where they had to learn in Georgian, though they knew only a few basic words. *Gamardjoba*, "hello"; *gmadlobt*, "thank you"; *me war*, "I am"; *diakh*, "yes"; *ara*, "no"; *dzma*, "brother." Nor did they like their new classmates, who mocked their ignorance of Georgian and never missed the opportunity to tease them as cruelly as possible.

Perhaps she should have been more concerned about their problems; perhaps she was too sure it would all sort itself out. She was actually pleased that the initial hostility and mockery the boys encountered at school brought them even closer together. Only years later did she realize that they never fought or quarreled. She couldn't remember either boy ever complaining to her about the other.

They were always there for each other. Shamil was very self-contained, calmer and quieter, with a thoughtful nature. Maybe that was why he seemed more capable than Rashid, though both of them did well in school. Shamil also had an authoritative character that prompted others to listen to him and do as he said.

Rashid was physically stronger, more powerfully built, and a little taller than Shamil. He was also quicker to flare up and to fight. Shamil was his guide in everything. Rashid trusted him on every matter, as if his brother were substituting for their absent father. One day at school, Rashid attacked an older boy who had thrown a punch at Shamil on the playground. The other boy was bigger and stronger, but he was helpless in the face of Rashid's blind rage. Rashid knocked him down and pounded his bleeding face until the teachers dragged him off. No one ever dared tease the brothers at school again, and gradually they got used to the new place. They also learned to speak Georgian, but despite not knowing it as well as the other children did, they impressed their teachers as the brightest and best students in the class.

The Kists were too busy with their everyday concerns and responsibilities to talk about the past, or to think about it, either. Whenever reminded of the life she'd left behind on the other side of the mountains, Lara was surprised to find how thoroughly she had wiped it from her mind, as if it were unimportant or had never happened.

The war had erupted very soon after they left Grozny, and hadn't ended in a few days or weeks—they couldn't have just sat it out. Lara was pleased that on arriving in Ingushetia, she had immediately decided not to stop there, living in a small corner at a friend's or relative's place, but to go straight home to Pankisi. Soon after they left, thousands of refugees came down to Karabulak from Grozny, where there was fighting on the streets and in public places. Every day more people came, and soon there wasn't enough room for them. Then the goodwill ran out, followed by the patience, taking the sympathy with it. Though at first the locals had taken in the evacuees willingly, now they couldn't wait to be rid of them. People glowered at them suspiciously, as if afraid they'd bring bad luck. But Lara and her children were already safe, on the other side of the mountains.

News of the war reached her through the television and was also brought by people who regularly traveled in the mountains, going as far as Chechnya. There were also some Kists who had gone to fight in Chechnya alongside their kinsmen and who had then come home from the insurgent camps to recover from illnesses or war wounds, and they brought news too.

Although Lara heard them talking about what had happened in Grozny, she couldn't imagine what they were describing. On New Year's Eve, downtown where her theater was located, Chechen insurgents had destroyed and set fire to a hundred Russian tanks. There were so many fires in the city at night that it was as bright as day. The presidential palace, which she and her sons had passed on their way home almost every day, had been blown up. Almost all the city's buildings had been damaged during the street fighting.

"What about the theater?" she'd asked. "Is it still standing?"

"The theater?" said the insurgent, newly arrived from Grozny.

He didn't know if the theater had survived, but then he hadn't known it was there at all. The men involved in the street fighting knew where barricades had been erected, who was fighting in which part of the city, who commanded which unit, and where they were billeted. But they had no idea which buildings had been where before the war.

The world of the past had been destroyed along with the city, invalidated by everything that had happened since. Lara understood that. Her only memories of Grozny predated the war, but for those who were there during the fighting, it existed only in its present shape. So Lara didn't ask about Minutka, where her old home had stood. It was meaningless by now.

The war dragged on, with neither side in the conflict gaining the upper hand. But the longer it continued, the more often people cursed the men who had started it.

People who had once been staunch supporters of the Chechen president, who had admired his courage and dedication and who had called for even stronger resistance to the Russians, now blamed him for the destruction, suffering, and homelessness caused by the war. Meanwhile, those who had always seen him as a troublemaker exposing them to danger in the name of the illusion of freedom were now cursing the Russians too. Instead of restoring peace and order, as they had promised, the Russians had changed their lives into endless misery.

The war was in its second year when the Russians finally tracked down the Chechen president in his mountain hideout and assassinated him. But just when they seemed about to crush the enemy, the Chechen insurgents reappeared like ghosts in the ruins of Grozny, recaptured it, and forced the Russians to agree to a cease-fire. In fact, it was a victory for the Chechens, because the Russian troops hadn't frightened them into laying down their weapons; instead, the Chechens had repulsed the enemy attack and were prepared to go on fighting. The Chechens were the only race in the Caucasus that hadn't surrendered to the Russians. This raised them above the rest, and only the Armenians and Ossetians were said to be their equals in the art of war. They were heroes again, admired again, and the Kists of the Pankisi Gorge were extremely proud to be their brothers.

They started traveling across the mountains again, to revel in the glory that was partly theirs too. They were the only Caucasian tribe to have stood shoulder to shoulder with the Chechens in a war that had seemed destined to failure. They also went to Grozny in search of work, because the city would have to be rebuilt but lacked laborers. Russia was to pay for the reconstruction of the devastated country. The period following a war is always a boom time for those who aren't afraid to start all over again.

And Lara made the trip too—not to look for work, but to see if she still felt at home in Grozny. Was there still a place for her there? she wondered. More to the point, was there a place for her sons? She felt a little guilty that by taking them away from there, she had deprived them of the touch of pride that came with being Chechen. Perhaps she'd been in too much of a hurry to escape and had yielded too readily to her fear? Perhaps she had lacked faith?

She went alone to find out for herself, leaving the boys at home in the care of their grandparents. She was afraid that if they came with her, she wouldn't be able to make a sober judgment. What if they liked the city before she had a chance to work out her own feelings about it? In Pankisi, everyone was talking nonstop about the Chechens and their victory; the exploits of the insurgents; their valor, bravery, and martyrdom. The names of the most famous commanders were endlessly repeated like the names of the saints in Orthodox churches. And all the children were playing at nothing but insurgents and war—her boys included.

The city terrified her. It was alien, hostile, aggressive, and at first unrecognizable. She'd been expecting it to be more badly ruined, but when she got off the bus in the city center, she had no trouble rediscovering the old, familiar places: the theater, Shamil's school, Rashid's kindergarten, and the park they used to cross on the way home. From a distance they looked intact. But when she got closer, she could see that walls that looked smooth and colorful from a distance had actually been cracked by bombs and pockmarked by gunfire. Most of the buildings were lifeless, shattered inside, their gaping windows charred by fire and smoke. The wide streets were littered with rubble, broken glass, bits of twisted metal, and scorched pieces of broken furniture thrown or dragged from the buildings. Even the trees in the park were badly damaged.

The plainest evidence of war was in the square outside the presidential palace. Ripped up by caterpillar tracks, explosions, shrapnel, and mortars, it was more like a potato field plowed for the winter than the smart, urban precinct of the past.

The palace itself, formerly the finest building in the city, a symbol of its splendor, now stood alone amid the crooked stumps of lampposts and charred trees. Until the insurgents had surrendered the city, the Chechen president had commanded the war from the palace basement. The Russians had tried their best to raze the building by bombing it from the air and shelling it from tanks and artillery. They must have been surprised that it survived such relentless bombardment.

A few blocks down from the presidential palace, the main road through the city led on to Minutka, and that was where Lara was heading. She wanted to see if her old house had survived. Was their apartment intact, she wondered, and was anyone living there? Since leaving Grozny, she'd had no news from her husband. She'd hadn't tried to find out what had happened to him, either. Making no decisions, she had left it to fate.

To tell the truth, she wasn't entirely sure what she was looking for in Grozny. She simply felt she must see it and that only then would she know exactly what to do next. If she felt she didn't belong there anymore, she'd abandon her final doubts and her sense of guilt and go home to the Pankisi Gorge. With that aim in mind, she set off to walk from the park outside the presidential palace to Minutka.

There were people wandering among the ruins, there were cars on the move and stalls up and running—life was slowly returning. Lara stopped outside the burned remains of the palace. Something made it impossible to walk past indifferently; it looked both pitiful and menacing. It was like a tombstone you can't pass without slowing down out of respect for the dead. Cracked and charred, with its roof caved in, it looked unstable, and Lara couldn't help thinking it was just about to come crashing down. As she gazed at the battered palace, she thought it looked more terrifying in its present state than it would have if it had actually collapsed.

"So who's this we have here?" she heard.

She hadn't noticed the military vehicle stopping just behind her, or the soldiers who were now standing around her.

"Where are you from and what are you looking for?" asked the soldier who appeared to be in charge. She didn't know what to say. She wasn't a stranger here, but she didn't feel local anymore, either.

"Are you a Russki?" he said in Russian.

"No, I'm a Chechen," she hastily replied in Chechen, quite frightened, as if he'd accused her of doing something wrong.

"A Chechen? You don't look local."

"I'm a Chechen from Georgia."

"Do Chechens live there?"

There were six of them. They were young and bearded, with long, tousled hair and swarthy complexions. They were smoking cigarettes. Only when she took a closer look did she notice that they were wearing randomly assembled uniforms. Two of them were in sneakers, and one was wearing jeans instead of army pants. They had no insignia or badges to show their military affiliation.

"And what's a Georgian Chechen doing here?" asked the commander.

"Taking a look around," she said.

"Taking a look around," he repeated, and she couldn't tell if he believed her.

She felt extremely scared, though there was nothing sinister in their faces to imply trouble. They were very young, not more than boys. The last time she had seen men with guns was when the war was still circling the city. Those men had been older, adults. She remembered the way they had clutched their rifles and the solemn, fearful expressions on their faces. They knew the war would be their business, but they didn't know what was involved or if they'd be able to cope.

These young men who had accosted her outside the charred remains of the presidential palace weren't afraid of war. They had been through it, they knew it well. Maybe that was why Lara found them so frightening. They carried their guns casually, slung around their necks or over their shoulders. They were laughing and joking, they were relaxed and confident. Before the war, she might have seen young men of this kind in the park, where they roamed around accosting young women—self-assured and pleased with themselves, as if the whole world belonged to them.

Their postwar contemporaries from outside the presidential palace clearly felt the same way. They had taken possession of the city by fighting in the war that had happened in its streets. No wonder they felt at home here—it was their city now, they owned it, they made the rules and the decisions. Lara figured they had won that right in the war, while others could at best be reconciled to the role of sublessees, who should be content with the right to remain permanently. By exposing their own lives to danger and by killing others, they had formed an exclusive brotherhood. And yet they prompted fear in her. She was sure that war must change people, and she was afraid of them. She didn't know what made them different from the people who fled from war, taking their children with them. How did these men feel? How did they think? Definitely not the same way, but how? Where did they draw the line between right and wrong, between what was allowed and what was not?

Apart from stories about the Chechen insurgents' noble exploits, she had also heard about an increasing tendency among the victors to take advantage of all the confusion to kidnap people for ransom. At first, no one believed this sort of news; when it kept being repeated, it was generally blamed on foreign volunteers who had come from the Arab world to join the holy war in defense of their Muslim brothers. There were also rumors that since resisting the mighty Russian army, many of the insurgent commanders were so self-confident that they no longer recognized any higher authority or laws.

"Go on then, take a look, Georgian Chechen," said the patrol commander at last. "And mind how you go. Who knows, perhaps we'll meet again one day."

Instead of going to Minutka, she went straight back to the place where she had stepped off the bus from Ingushetia that morning and where she could catch another one for the return journey. When some military vehicles full of long-haired, bearded young insurgents drove past, Lara thought she could see the men who had accosted her outside the palace. She quickened her pace, as if to escape the feeling that they were coming after her every step of the way. This was their city, and she felt like an intruder in it.

Another memory she retained of this final visit to Grozny was that the ordinary people in the streets seemed strange— cowering, fearful, vigilant, ready to run away. She felt that the longer she stayed there, the more that terror would infect her and strip away her confidence.

"I didn't want my boys to grow up like them. Or like the young men outside the palace, either," Lara said pensively. "It wasn't a good place to bring up children."

In the McDonald's, two girls with school bags over their shoulders were standing at the top of the stairs, holding red plastic trays and hesitantly looking around the empty restaurant. Lara and I were the only people there.

"Where shall we sit?" asked the taller girl. "Would you rather be by the window or over there, in the corner?"

"Either. Just so we can have a quiet chat," said the other one, shrugging and casting us a mistrustful glance. "Maybe by the window."

They sat at a table overlooking Rustaveli Avenue and the subway entrance. They looked like close friends wanting to swap news and offer each other advice in private. At first sight, they could have been sisters or cousins. They had the same long, raven-black hair; petite, slender figures; dark eyes; and oval faces like the Madonna from an icon. They were also dressed alike, in the latest fashion. They took their drinks, boxes of sandwiches, salads, fries, and desserts off their trays and put them on the table, forming a cardboard pyramid.

"So are you gonna tell me?" the taller girl urged, taking out a cell phone.

"Hold on a mo', I can't find it . . ." the other one replied, running a finger down her phone screen.

"Okay, I've got it. See for yourself!"

They both went quiet, staring at their phones and tapping their thumbs on the keyboards. Without speaking or looking up, they reached for the sandwiches and fries lying on the table.

Lara seemed so engrossed in what was going on at the girls' table that she seemed to have forgotten I was there. This had happened earlier too. It didn't take much for her to fly off in her thoughts; for her, the present moment was just a shifting border she often crossed. This time I was afraid we'd never get back to our conversation—that's what the absent look on her face seemed to imply.

"You didn't want your sons to grow up in the city . . ." I prompted her. "You said the city wasn't a good . . ."

"The war was still there," she said mechanically, forcing herself to pick up the thread. "People think they can escape from something like that."

And so, the war that Lara had run away from twice didn't forget about her, but followed her across the mountains. In no time, it had caught up with her.

Though they'd failed to beat the Chechens at the first blow, the Russians had no intention of accepting defeat. They withdrew, but only to wait for the chance to strike again. They watched patiently for the moment when the Chechens would fall out, start fighting each other, and squander the admiration and sympathy that others felt for them. They wasted their own victory, which went to their heads like dark Kindzmarauli wine, distorting their view of the world.

The Russians brought a new war to the Caucasus when the Chechens were at their weakest; by now they had alienated all their neighbors with their pride, aggression, and love of violence, and could no longer rely on anybody's help, military backup, or mercy.

This time the Russians didn't send infantry or tank divisions to storm the city, but calmly bombarded it from the air, using cannon, mortars, rocket launchers, and flamethrowers of every caliber. They only advanced once the besieged city lay in ruins and deathly silence reigned.

With no need to hurry, they attacked slowly, reducing the whole place to ashes. This time, on their approach to Grozny, they didn't leave the population an escape route as they had before. Instead, Grozny's defenders were forced to pay the surrounding enemy a huge ransom to get out of the burning city. And even then, they were cheated, because the field the Russians told the Chechens they could cross safely at night turned out to be riddled with land mines. Afterward, the Russians claimed ignorance, saying that the Chechens must have laid the mines themselves during the previous war.

Those who managed to escape sought refuge in the mountains by following the rivers up toward their sources. But the Russians weren't satisfied with capturing the steppes above the Terek River, razing Grozny, and occupying Chechnya's highland *auls*. Hot on the heels of the fleeing Chechens, they climbed up the Argun River valley, sending their air force ahead, until the refugees were forced into a snow-covered pass leading across the ice-bound peaks to the other side of the mountains. Winter was in full force. Nothing was visible in the mist-filled ravines on the southern slopes but the soaring stone towers, built centuries ago. Far below, roads and paths wound between them, leading to the gorges occupied by Georgian highlanders and to the home of the Kists, a little farther beyond. That was where the refugees were heading.

Lara couldn't remember when the first of them arrived in her village, or who they were. Suddenly, almost overnight, the gorge was full of people, and with each new day, more of them arrived, on heavily laden trucks, in cars, on overburdened horses and on foot. Men and women, old and young, children too. With parcels and bundles, wrapped in blankets to keep out the cold. They also brought their sick and wounded. They came to a halt in the village, waiting for the locals to gather round and ask them questions, then take pity on their misfortune and homelessness, invite them in, feed them, and offer them accommodation.

Soon there wasn't a house in Jokolo, or in the entire Pankisi Gorge, where the Kists had failed to take in a Chechen family. They gave them the upstairs guest rooms and even the porches—heated and suitably adapted, they made a good temporary living space.

The local kindergarten, the firehouse, and the mosque in Duisi were also assigned to the refugees, as were the public offices; as no instructions or money for salaries had been sent from Tbilisi for some time, they weren't being used anyway. The homeless Chechens filled every corner, and by the end of winter, when the mountain pastures were starting to go green, there were more newcomers in the gorge than locals.

As well as refugees there were also insurgents—freedom fighters hung about with rifles, bazookas, grenades, and ammunition belts. By mingling with the escaping civilians, they thought they could hide from the Russian planes. But the pilots never stopped to consider who was traveling in the vehicles that went racing up the steep roads into the mountains. They simply followed orders and fired at all of them. To them, any Chechen, civilian or armed, was a bloodthirsty thug; they were all the enemy. So the insurgents had traveled among the civilians on equal terms, unable to insist on the precedence due to troops during a war. They didn't hurry the civilians or push them out of the way, though they were in a rush to get across the mountains before the Russians dropped a landing force on the border and blocked the pass. Then they would have to retreat into the mountains to hide from the planes and helicopters, and spend the winter sheltering in caves. Or disband their units in the hope of wintering in the villages, and then return to their mountain camps in spring. They weren't thrilled by either prospect, so they were hurrying to reach the pass before the Russians got there.

The Chechens weren't afraid of the Georgian border guards, who didn't try to stop them or force them to give up their weapons before entering Georgian territory. They knew that at best the Chechens would laugh at them, and that at worst they'd aim their guns at them.

Although Georgia was gradually recovering from its own wars, it was still struggling to lift itself out of poverty and lawlessness, and few people in the Caucasus were afraid of the Georgian military. They had lost their wars against the Abkhazians and the Ossetians, and they'd had a civil war too. Defeated on every front, the authorities had had to ask the Russians for help. So when the Chechen insurgents appeared on the border, the Georgians simply turned a blind eye to them.

The insurgents who took up residence in Jokolo seemed to Lara older than the ones she'd seen in Grozny. Maybe because they had longer hair and beards, or maybe because of the battles they'd fought and their difficult journey across the mountains. Or perhaps defeat had left its mark on their faces.

One day, as she and her sons were coming back from the marketplace in Duisi, she noticed an insurgent in the street who looked familiar. She wanted to go up to him and ask questions, but in no time, he disappeared among the market traders. On the way home in her brother's car, she saw him again through the window. The soldier was standing with several others, dressed alike, in an army jacket and a black woolen cap. It must have been an illusion, but briefly Lara thought she recognized him as the commander of the patrol that had stopped her outside the ruined presidential palace in Grozny. Just as then, she felt a chill come over her. She glanced round at her sons in the backseat, but they took no notice. They were looking the other way.

A few days later, the insurgents brought a wounded man called Omar to Lara's house in Jokolo, where two Chechen refugee families were already staying. In fact, it was Ali, her cousin, who brought him there. Ali had left home as soon as news of the war in Chechnya reached the Pankisi Gorge. Just after graduating from high school, he had joined the insurgents and fought in the same unit as Omar.

Omar was much older, almost forty. He was originally from the valley too, but had left it many years ago. When the first Chechen war erupted, he was in Siberia, where he had gone to earn a living. He had been successful there, gained a degree in engineering, got a well-paid job at a meat processing plant, married, and started a family. And yet, as soon as he heard about the war threatening Chechnya, he had dropped everything, returned to the Caucasus, and volunteered for the Chechen forces.

After the first, victorious war, he had decided not to return to Siberia, but to wait a little longer, until the situation was fully resolved, and then find a house in Grozny, set up a business, bring in his family, and spend the rest of his life in the Caucasus.

But the war came back, and Omar's plans were blown sky-high, along with the city. It was from him that Lara learned that her own former home in Grozny had been destroyed.

Omar had been wounded in the building where she had once lived. Minutka was the last line of defense for the Chechens, who posted snipers in the windows of the multistory blocks towering over it, to hold back the enemy attacking from the city center. The Russians had razed half the city, but rather than destroy the tower blocks, they wanted to capture them to use as their own guard towers, in case the Chechens ever launched a counterattack.

The Russians had forced their way up to the tower blocks, but they couldn't drive the Chechens out of them. The insurgents put up a defense from the higher stories, while the Russian soldiers attacked from below. By night, through secret underground tunnels, more insurgents came to help their besieged comrades, trapping the Russians between them. The stairs and corridors were soon piled with corpses, and the air was acrid with the smell of gunpowder.

The heaviest fighting had occurred in the tallest tower block, where Lara and her family had lived on the tenth floor. It was right there, on the staircase two floors lower down, that Omar was wounded by shots from a high-caliber rifle. The soldier who fired at him must have been hiding on the floor above, because the bullets had ripped across Omar's body, from his neck to his belly. Afterward, the doctors who saved his life saw his survival as miraculous; none of the bullets had broken his spine, although at least one had damaged it, depriving him of sensation.

The Chechens had only abandoned the fight when they started to run out of ammunition, and were ordered to retreat by their leaders, who, one after another, slipped out of the city to hide in the mountains. To give them time to escape, the remaining commanders held off the Russians for as long as possible. Finally they too saw that continuing the fight would mean certain death.

The wounded Omar had been carried out of the city by the last insurgents to withdraw. They left at night, in a blizzard, across a field toward a village named Alkhan-Kala. But the escape route turned out to be a trap—the field was mined. More Chechen insurgents were killed or disabled that night than in almost one hundred days of fighting for the city. Yet Omar survived. His comrades carried him over the mountains, all the way to the hospital in Tbilisi for surgery. Only there did he start to move his legs again and, later on, to walk. But his injuries were so extensive and he had lost so much blood that the doctors gave him little chance of survival.

When Omar was discharged from the hospital, his comrades had taken him to the Pankisi Gorge. Although he came from the valley, he had no home of his own there, and his relatives' house was already hosting refugee families. So Ali, who had been in the same unit as Omar, brought him to Lara's house.

She refused to take him in.

"That's all I need!" she protested. "The house is already packed. And the last thing I want is a strange man in the house! What will people say?"

But Ali finally managed to persuade her that nobody would think badly of her for taking in a wounded man.

"The doctors say he won't last long," he explained. "Let the man die like a human being. He deserves at least that much from life."

She agreed, but what choice did she have?

They organized a separate room for him on the porch at the back of the house, by covering the floor with felt blankets to make a bed. Ali brought in a cast-iron stove and attached a metal flue that he fed through the window. Omar was too weak to carry firewood himself, so Lara made sure the fire in his stove didn't go out. Sometimes she sent her sons to the porch to see if it was still going and to ask if he needed anything.

They never came straight back. And whenever they disappeared or didn't answer her call, she knew they were sitting on the porch, engrossed in Omar's tales of the war. She also knew where to find them if they left the house for longer than usual and didn't come back for dinner. Like the other children, they spent their time in the old warehouse, the closed depot for agricultural machinery, or at the kindergarten assigned to the newly arrived insurgents as living quarters.

The schools were closed for the season, so the children had nothing to do and nowhere to go. There was usually a break in their studies in winter because of the cold weather and frequent power cuts that made it impossible to heat the classrooms. Sometimes the teachers weren't paid, and didn't return to the gorge after the Christmas vacation, so the students had to wait for new ones to be sent from Tbilisi. Now the refugees from the first Chechen war had arrived and had to be given somewhere to live.

Drawn by curiosity, the local kids hung around the houses where Chechen families were living, but what attracted them most of all were the insurgents. The boys in particular could spend hours on end silently watching them, listening to their conversations, staring at their shining, greased rifles, and breathing in their metallic smell. They'd leap up and race to be first whenever one of the insurgents asked a favor. Usually this meant running to the nearest store for cigarettes or cookies. Overjoyed at being chosen, they filled their pockets with the small change the insurgents let them keep.

The boldest children sometimes dared to ask the insurgents to tell them about the war, what had happened to them and what they had seen. Lara's sons could listen to these stories endlessly. Without hiding their irritation, they would drag their heels whenever she came to fetch them home. "Just a little longer, two minutes," they'd beg her. They resented her for treating them like children. "Don't come to fetch us, or the others will laugh at us," they said. Shamil was fourteen now, and Rashid was eleven. On the way home they'd be full of it all, discussing the stories they'd heard. They'd debate which rifle was better in combat, which insurgent commander was the bravest, and under whose command they'd like to serve. Here they were in agreement. All the boys in the valley regarded Ruslan Gelayev as the best, bravest, and wisest commander. But everyone called him Hamzat, the name he had adopted after his pilgrimage to

Mecca. The insurgents quartered in the valley were from his unit. His men included the wounded Omar and Lara's cousin Ali. In the past, Gelayev had commanded more than a thousand men, but only a hundred at most had survived the war and the journey across the mountains. Gelayev himself was living with a local family. Lara had seen him a few times on the road. Tall, with broad shoulders and a long beard, he dressed in black. He had a son Shamil's age, and the boys were excited to think that soon he'd be at school with them.

As she walked after her sons, listening to them discuss the war and the insurgents, once again Lara found herself wondering if she had fled the war too soon. If she had stayed in Grozny a little longer, the boys would have seen for themselves what war was like—it would have been a good thing for them to be properly terrified by it. It would certainly have frightened them. Lara was sure she would feel much calmer if they didn't admire the insurgents so much and weren't gaining a romantic image of war from their tales of heroes and martyrs.

Sometimes the insurgents gave the children small souvenirs: hardtack from their military rations, sugar lumps, or apples. But the most prized treasures were gifts related to the war and the army: uniform buttons, buckles, insignia, woolen caps, gloves, real bullets, or cartridge cases.

One day, the boys came running home with an army bayonet they'd been given by the insurgents. They proudly laid it on the kitchen table and unwrapped it from an oily piece of cloth with reverence, as if it were a holy relic. Then, uncharacteristically, they immediately began to quarrel over whose gift it was and who had the greater right to own it.

Without a word, Lara picked up the heavy bayonet. The boys stared at her as if at a complete stranger. She said that as long as she lived and breathed, she'd never let the war or any of its scrap iron come inside her house. The boys didn't answer, but Lara could see barely concealed anger, if not hostility, in their eyes for the first time ever—as if she had deprived them of something that had special meaning because it marked them out from all the other boys. Though nothing like it ever happened again, this incident sank deep into Lara's memory.

"Are we Muslims?" asked her younger son, Rashid.

After supper, Lara was busy tidying the kitchen, but she heard her son's voice as clearly as if he were in the same room. She felt her cheeks go hot as the blood rushed to her head. Among the Kists, it was unacceptable for children to address the adults without being spoken to. In their father's presence, they were not allowed to quarrel or even cry. This sort of behavior was seen as proof that their parents had brought them up badly.

Lara peeked through the half-open door into the dining room, where her father and brothers were still sitting at the table with a neighbor who had dropped in on an errand and stayed for supper. Shamil and Rashid were sitting on the couch, watching television. In the customary way among the Kists, the men and women ate their meals apart, in separate rooms.

"Are we Muslims?" Rashid asked again.

She couldn't see him on the couch in front of the television set—he must have gone up to the table.

"Yes, Muslims, what else could we be?" She heard her father's irritated voice. "Don't you know that?"

"But Muslims pray differently from us," replied Rashid.

"Differently? Where did you get that idea from?"

"The Chechens said so. They said we do it wrong. Not honestly."

"Rashid! Shamil!" Lara called through the door. "I need help. Go and fetch wood for the stove! I'm not going to do the carrying."

The boys put on their coats and went to the woodshed for logs; meanwhile, as she washed the dishes, Lara listened through the door to her father and the neighbor complaining about young people. And about the Chechens.

"They go to war against Russia, but they can't say a single sentence without sticking a Russki word in it. As if they didn't have a language of their own."

"Because they've forgotten it. Not surprising! Before the war they were all desperate to go and live in the cities—where every second person's a Russki. The fact is we Kists have more of a right to call ourselves Chechens than they do. We speak purer Chechen than the so-called Chechens. Apparently the city folk speak Russian all the time at home. And they live like Russkis, not like Caucasians."

"Here we live the old way, like our ancestors. But how can you live like a Caucasian in the city?"

"Very true. They forget the old customs, and they have no respect for their elders."

"And that's the cause of all the trouble. When people don't respect the sacred traditions, they don't respect themselves, either. And if you don't respect yourself, you don't respect anything. Nothing will give them peace or satisfaction, they'll just go on fighting to the death."

A lighter clicked, and the smell of cigarettes came floating into the kitchen.

"Yes, just look at the children! They're already telling us we don't live honestly, we don't know how to pray."

"Those guys are confusing them, stirring them up. They've got all the answers. You're not allowed to smoke tobacco, not allowed to drink wine, not allowed to eat sausage, either. 'Don't do this, don't do that'; nothing's allowed."

"If it goes any further, they'll turn the whole lot of us into Arabs, not Russkis."

The door opened, and a gust of fresh air and damp snow blew in from the hall. Shamil and Rashid dropped armfuls of logs onto the floor and started stacking them by the stove.

"What got into you to say those things to the adults?" Lara asked angrily. "And who told you that?"

"That's what they say," Shamil replied.

"'They'? Who are 'they'?"

"The Chechens," Shamil explained.

"The ones living at the kindergarten?"

"Yes. But so do the boys who go to school with us. They say that at our mosque, nothing's done the right way."

"So, they're the experts, are they?" She shrugged.

"They say we should be learning Arabic, because the Koran is written in Arabic."

"Here we learn our faith from our fathers."

"But Grandpa can't speak Arabic. So, how does he know what it says in the Koran?"

"And did you know there are Arabs in our village too? I saw two of them at the kindergarten. They know a bit of Chechen," said Rashid. "The Prophet Mohammed was an Arab, did you know that?"

She nodded.

"And do you know what they say about the way we pray here?" her younger son asked.

"What?"

"We're like puppets!" Both boys burst out laughing. "They say that during prayers we jump up and run around in circles; we look like the dolls at the puppet theater. They say real Muslims don't pray like that, and Allah doesn't like our sort of prayers."

Arguments about who did and did not have the right to call themselves a real Muslim were becoming more common in Pankisi. Once the Chechens had shaken off their war-induced depression and gotten used to the gorge and to their hosts, they openly began to point out the Kists' backward, out-of-date practices, as they saw it, and their mistaken views about the world around them.

Even if the Chechens only had their brothers' best interests at heart and believed that by being honest they could save them from making the wrong choices, the Kists took it as an outrageous lack of ceremony, highly inappropriate behavior by guests enjoying their hospitality, and extremely bad manners.

What was wrong with them living as their fathers had? They saw no reason to cast off or change the old customs. They hadn't invented them, nor were they going to judge them. These practices had been established over the centuries and generations. If they really were a burden, leading to doom, they'd have been dropped long ago. But it was these traditions that had shaped the Kists and given them their identity. They helped them to remember who they were, even among strangers in a foreign land. They had survived, while many other Caucasian ethnicities had vanished and been forgotten long ago. So their role wasn't to pursue the latest trends, but to remember how they had lived for generations, and to pass this wisdom down to their sons and grandsons as an inheritance that would keep them from disappearing or losing their way too.

Even in the periods when they'd been subordinate to foreign powers, they had always managed their own affairs, according to their own rules. They had drawn their own lines between good and bad, found their own way of resolving both minor and major disputes, and made their own judgments about crime, punishment, and compensation. They never summoned the Georgian police, investigative magistrates, or judges if they could find and judge the culprits themselves, whether guilty of murder, robbery, or marital infidelity. This ability was especially useful in the toughest times, during the historical storms that threatened to annihilate them, during Georgia's civil war, for instance, when lawlessness and poverty were rife. Entirely forgotten, they'd have failed miserably if they had pinned their salvation on nothing but the goodwill of others. Instead of making a futile appeal for aid, they had found useful pointers in the memory of how they had lived in the past. While violence and disorder reigned in Tbilisi, Mingrelia, and Imereti, in the Pankisi Gorge the Kist elders took over the administration, and life continued according to the old rules and customs.

The Kists had put their lives in the hands of the elders, men who were brave, honest, and wise. Just like other Caucasian highlanders, the Kists believed that the experience gathered during a long life gave them wisdom just as valuable as the knowledge gained through academic study. The elders were regarded as authorities on every matter, their word was final, and the young people should always respect and obey them.

Even before the Chechen refugees arrived, the Kist elders were aware that they weren't as knowledgeable about Islam as they were about the old customs and laws. They didn't know Arabic, so they hadn't read the Koran in the original, and only a few of them had a copy of it, translated into Russian or Georgian. They didn't even know it was a mortal sin to attempt to translate the words of the Prophet into a foreign language. They weren't free to travel abroad to study Islam at the famous academies in Cairo, Damascus, or Jerusalem. To go on a pilgrimage to Mecca, they would have to register at a special office, then wait for permission and for a passport issued only for the period of the trip. Anyway, there had been no question of them going to Mecca or a Muslim academy in the days when the authorities in their country claimed that God did not exist, when they had closed down places of worship and jailed the priests. The believers prayed at home, where they set aside a room for prayer. But this furtive form of worship was also frowned upon and could bring trouble and persecution.

So the Kist elders didn't claim the right to resolve matters of faith, but accepted instead that the young people were far better informed about it than they were. They were living in a new world now, where there weren't supposed to be any borders. They were free to travel, follow any faith, and do whatever they liked. Their elders were afraid that the sudden freedom their people had gained might turn against them. But despite their mistrust of change and novelty, they accepted that the dangers brought by the new and unfamiliar times were extremely small compared with the many advantages they promised.

The older Kists didn't object when the younger ones went to study far away, nowadays not just in Russia but in Europe too. Very few families in the gorge could afford a European education, but more and more of the young Kists were heading off to Turkey, Egypt, Syria, Jordan, and even Saudi Arabia, land of the Prophet, where their studies were paid for by local benefactors who saw it as their duty to help Muslims from other countries and to show them the truths revealed by Islam. Arab emissaries touring the world as pilgrims came to the gorge too, and encouraged the Kists to travel to the Middle East. They had arrived in Chechnya much earlier on.

When the young Kists came home for the holidays or after finishing their studies, the older generation was happy to listen to their stories from the world outside. The young ones shared news and the knowledge they had gained, and those who had been to Arab colleges explained how to find the path to salvation and how not to deviate from it. The older people saw no harm in these stories. On the contrary, they seemed to bring nothing but advantages; it never occurred to the young people that the wisdom they'd gained abroad could be used to rebel against their elders or against the rules they upheld.

So it was—until the Chechens arrived in Pankisi Gorge. By sneering at the Kists' old customs, they began to set the young against the old, stirring them up and talking them round to their way of thinking. "Faith is truth, and you'll find the answer to every question in the Koran, and pointers to steer you through life toward salvation. You should be guided by them and them alone, and not by the words of old men, who can't be good guides because they have no idea about the truth and don't even try to seek it. Don't bow down to your elders, but to God. Show your obeisance to Him—you owe it to no one but Him alone. Have you sworn allegiance to the elders just because they've lived to a great age? No custom, not even the oldest, can take priority over the truth of faith. Customs are invented by people, but faith comes from the Almighty. Whom do you serve? God or the elders?" said the Chechens, especially the insurgents and their mullahs, to persuade the young Kists. The insurgents called themselves mujahideen, holy warriors. "You sit in this gorge," they said, "shut away, knowing nothing about the world or how it's changing. No one lives the way you do anymore."

Many of the young Kists thought the Chechens and their priests were right. They started wondering if anyone who was so wrong about matters of faith could really be an authority in everything else. First covertly and then, encouraged by the mujahideen, more openly, they began to question the wisdom of the elders and to undermine their right to superior status.

Deeply offended, the old men decided to bar the rebels from their mosques. So, without a second thought, the Chechens started building one of their own. Without asking permission, they built it faster than anyone might have expected. It was in Duisi, the largest village in the gorge, on the main road, next to the middle school. Compared with the Kists' hundred-year-old mosque, it looked like a palace—large, of red brick, with a minaret covered in silvery metal; next door, it had a madrassa for religious instruction, a house for the imam, and an Arabic language school. This mosque and then others were constructed at the expense of the Arab emissaries, more and more of whom were arriving in the gorge. They came with aid for the refugees, their brothers in faith, to give them spiritual support, but also to energize the insurgents to continue the fight. Volunteers for war in the mountains, mainly Arabs, also arrived from abroad. There were even rumors that Osama bin Laden, regarded as the emir of the mujahideen worldwide, was planning to slip into the gorge and hide from his oppressors there and then use it as a command base for his global holy war.

At the new redbrick mosque, gifts sent by Arab benefactors were distributed. Although anyone living in the gorge could come and take them, almost all the gifts ended up in the possession of the people who came here to pray or to sit in the courtyard all day long, swapping stories and trying to kill time, which they all had in excess.

Lara's sons also sat outside the new mosque with the other boys. This was where the most interesting things happened locally. They'd gaze at the bearded insurgents who came to pray, and they'd listen in on their conversations and stories. For the Chechens, time dragged slowly, so to amuse themselves and keep fit, they practiced hand-to-hand combat and lifted weights in the mosque courtyard. The boys copied every move, and sometimes the insurgents yielded to their pleas to show them how to throw punches and also how to parry them. And when the imam handed out the foreign gifts, he made sure none of the boys went home without one.

One day, Lara's sons asked her to shorten their pants to ankle length, the way the imam from the new mosque and the Prophet himself wore them. She refused, explaining that if their pants were too short, they'd look funny.

"All right, I'll cut them short myself!" Shamil said angrily.

"Just you try, and you'll be sorry!" she replied.

"You can't talk to me like that!" he shouted. "I'm fifteen years old, and I'm grown up. That's what the imam says. I'm a man now, and you can't tell me what to do anymore."

To her own surprise, instead of flying into a rage, she burst out laughing. Her response to her son's insolence wasn't anger, but amusement. She went up to him and ruffled his hair.

"My grown-up man," she said. "My defender."

He tore free from her, jumping back as if scalded.

"Stop it, Mom!" he cried.

"What about you?" she said, putting her arms around Rashid and pressing him tightly to her chest. "Are you a grown-up man already too?"

Lara's father had warned her against letting her sons spend so much time at the new mosque. She had brushed off his concerns with assurances that she'd deal with it, but in fact she wasn't particularly worried about her sons going to the new mosque and associating with the people they met there. She thought the old men were exaggerating when they said those people were black sheep who disrespected everything sacred and were trying to destroy the old world. She liked the fact that they prohibited smoking and drinking, and also drugs, which hadn't been a problem in the gorge until recently. They said that surrendering to these weaknesses was a sin, unacceptable for real Muslims.

One day, the young men from the new mosque stopped a man on the main road whom everyone locally knew to be a smuggler. They dragged him out of his car, searched it, and found some drugs. In sight of the entire village, they threw the package into the river, although the old men protested, saying it was worth a fortune that could benefit everyone in the gorge. The young men also did what they could to rescue drug addicts. They shut themselves in the mosque with the addicts and spent days on end praying until their patients felt permanently free of the temptation.

They formed their own civil militia and set out on patrols to track down criminals in the gorge. Anyone they caught was taken to the new mosque, where in the presence of the imam they were tried and penalized according to Koranic law. This, too, the Kist elders saw as an attack on their authority and on their old, traditional laws.

Lara didn't think the young men at the mosque could lead her sons astray. She liked their austerity and simplicity, their appeals for purification and renewal of faith. What about their belligerence and their extreme moral principles verging on fanaticism? Lara saw them as a privilege of youth, when grand dreams, exaggerated views, and strong emotions were quite normal, not offensive or apparently dangerous.

But she did agree with her father that there was something unsettling in the air, a feverish mood that made it hard to feel lighthearted. Busy with their daily affairs, the locals didn't take notice, or failed to register the outwardly minor incidents that in time would turn out to be milestones in their lives. But the visitors could clearly see how the world of the unsuspecting Kists was turning upside down and dying.

The civil servants, policemen, and other officials who had administered local life until now were abandoning the gorge. It's not clear if they left of their own accord, out of fear of the Chechen insurgents, or if they were driven out. The fact was that the Chechens were taking control. With their beards and long hair, they didn't stay out of sight anymore, but sporting their rifles, they paraded around the streets and marketplaces.

After the officials left, as usual at a time of crisis, the Kist elders tried to establish their own administration, but few people listened to them. Their governing body couldn't do much, either, because matters were settled by the insurgents now, everything depended on them, and the final word belonged to their emir, Gelayev.

The authority of the elders and local respect for them were further diminished by the young people from the new mosque and their tribunal, which investigated complaints and settled disputes faster and at no cost, citing God's law and equality before Allah, regardless of wealth, connections, or merit.

The elders tried to defend themselves. Not against the faith—after all, they thought of themselves as Muslims. They were surprised by the sudden devotion that had come down from the mountains onto the local youth along with the war and its refugees. They were angry that the young upstarts from the new mosque and their mullahs were throwing their weight around. They also resented the Chechen visitors for repaying their hospitality with such ingratitude. So the elders and other defenders of the old order wrote complaints and appeals to the authorities in Tbilisi, calling for them to prevent the imams at the new mosque from teaching the children Arabic and sending them to study for free at schools and colleges in the Middle East. But all in vain—neither their requests nor their threats were answered. No one in the capital cared about the gorge or the fate of its residents, and nobody wanted to deal with the Chechens, insurgents, mullahs, and Arab emissaries who had settled there. In those days, it was hard to find a cab driver in Tbilisi who would agree to take a passenger to the gorge. The bravest or the most desperate would only drive as far as Akhmeta, the last Georgian town at the gateway to the gorge. Beyond there, you had to find your own way.

Thanks to the prevalent power vacuum, the gorge became a refuge for all sorts of villains. Here nobody kept an eye on them or came after them. The insurgents were too busy preparing for new military expeditions across the mountains, and the absence of Georgian officials, judges, policemen, and soldiers left a void. The insurgents treated the gorge like an army camp, setting up posts on the roads leading into it and refusing to admit anyone whom they found suspicious. The Georgian authorities preferred not to know what was going on among the Kists, especially as they didn't have the power to stop it.

Although it had put its own wars behind it, Georgia still wasn't coping with freedom, which had taken on the awkward form of self-aggrandizement and immunity from punishment. The police robbed travelers on the roads, and everyone had to pay bribes to officials and judges for settling the most minor matters. Even at schools, the teachers demanded payment for awarding good grades or for admission to a higher class. Everything was for sale, while the authorities had the best guarantee of money through access to the state treasury, fueled by loans and donations from the West. Europe and America had chosen Georgia as an ally and were treating it as their private bridgehead and trading post in the Caucasus.

So Georgia's political clans and parties were furiously jockeying for position as close as possible to the throne, fighting over every scrap of power. In the forgotten gorge, which had suddenly found itself outside anyone's control, venal officials from the capital spotted an opportunity for illicit business deals and an extra source of income.

The astounded Kists watched in alarm as convoys smuggling weapons, drugs, contraband, stolen cars, and herds of cattle passed through their villages. The country's most dangerous criminals, on the run from arrest warrants or revenge, saw the gorge as a safe place to hide, and kidnappers saw it as a good place to hide their hostages. There was no one to harass them, because the Georgian police were afraid to set foot here, and when they ventured too far, they were usually taken captive, obliging the authorities to pay a ransom for them. Kidnappings became such a plague that nobody in Georgia could feel safe. Even some Georgian government ministers were abducted and held in cellars in Kist villages. When news of the situation in the gorge became widespread, the authorities in Tbilisi were essentially helpless and could do nothing but establish police checkpoints on the roads leading into the gorge, with orders not to allow any nonresidents to enter the villages.

The smugglers, kidnappers, thieves, and killers were out-siders—Georgians, Armenians, Chechens, and even Russians. But it was the Kists who were on the receiving end of all the Georgians' hatred. Nor had the Georgians forgotten that when war erupted in their country, the Kists' brothers, the Chechens, had fought on the side of their enemies.

In this period, Lara never left the gorge, but neighbors and friends would return from trips to Tbilisi or Telavi and describe the hostility they had encountered there. As soon as they were recognized as Kists, clerks and store assistants, even hospital nurses, would respond in monosyllables, casting hos-tile glances. To the Georgians, a Kist was no better than a thug, a lowdown traitor, a fanatic, and a brute. A boy from Birkiani who was studying to be a doctor at the university in Tbilisi was beaten up by the other students purely because he came from the Pankisi Gorge. Lara was very upset about it, because her older son was due to go to secondary school soon. The local high school in Duisi had never had a good reputation, and in any case, at that point the gorge was not the best place for education, or for life in general. Shamil's teachers couldn't praise him highly enough, saying how talented he was and that he mustn't go to waste. Lara was considering sending him to school in Tbilisi. She had just about made up her mind and was asking around to see if any of her neighbors had family or friends in the city with whom Shamil could lodge during his studies. When she heard about the student from Birkiani who was beaten up, she started having doubts again.

The Georgians had stopped thinking of the Kists as compa-triots; it was also clear now that the Chechens didn't fully accept them, either. Everyone had begun to back away from them. The Chechens had sought salvation from the war in Pankisi Gorge, but now anyone who could was leaving it, scared off by insurgents, mullahs, Arabs, and, finally, by common criminals. There was a sense of actual war in the air too, as if it were just waiting for the right moment to strike. It hadn't stayed on the other side of the mountains after all.

Ignoring the presence of Georgian soldiers on the border, Russian planes and helicopters often came as far as the Pankisi Gorge, strafing the forest-covered mountainsides with missiles. They were targeting Chechen insurgent camps, but these air raids also killed shepherds and people gathering chestnuts and brushwood. The Russians bombed the village of Girevi, high in the mountains, and the Ilto River Valley in Tianeti, probably mistaking it for the Pankisi Gorge, which lies farther east. But they also dropped bombs in the forests surrounding Omalo and Birkiani, very close to Jokolo, where Lara and her sons lived.

The Georgian president came in person from Tbilisi for the funeral of one of the shepherds killed in a Russian raid. About a thousand people attended the funeral service, which was held at a small Orthodox church in the Georgian village of Matani. Some Kists came too, though for a long time now, because of the young people at the new mosque, they hadn't been going to the Georgian churches or attending Orthodox ceremonies. But the entire gorge wanted to see and hear the president for themselves.

He said the Russians had dropped the bombs, and that they had acted illegally and immorally; he had received a stream of messages from kings, presidents, and prime ministers the world over, expressing their sympathy, outrage, and support. He asked the residents of the gorge not to lose heart, and he appealed to the Chechens who had sheltered there from the war in their own country to return home. They could leave their old people, women, and children in the valley, and also the sick and wounded—help would be provided for them all. But the men should leave.

Everyone at the church, probably including the president himself, was fully aware that the insurgents would do as they wished and weren't afraid of the Georgian authorities. Nor were they scared of Russia, though the president threatened that if the Russians dared attack Georgian territory one more time, they would bitterly regret the act, because the Georgians would pay them back in kind. At these words, the mourners in the church simply smiled sadly.

In reply, the Russian president and his generals accused the Georgian leader of having lost control of his own capital and said his country was in a state of chaos. If he was incapable of restoring order and ridding Georgia of its uninvited Chechen guests, Russia would send across not just aircraft, but infantry too. Perhaps he had invited the Chechens into his country— that would mean he was harboring criminals who posed a threat not just to Russia but to the entire world. Helping villains would make him one of them.

A lot had changed in the world since the Chechens had lost the war against Russia and taken shelter among the Kists across the Georgian border. At that point, they could still count on sympathy and kindness from Europe and America. But they had lost their help when supporters of the holy war hijacked the passenger planes and launched their frenzied attacks on New York City and Washington. In retaliation, the West had sworn to fight the jihadists to the death. "Either you are with us, or you are with the terrorists," the American president declared. Russia immediately took his side, proclaiming the Chechen insurgents their enemies, jihadists and criminals as bad as Osama bin Laden. As the Americans awarded themselves the right to pursue and fight their enemies in any corner of the world, the Russians saw no reason why they shouldn't deal with their own foe in just the same way.

The Georgians wanted to be on the Western side too, believing that if they were counted as Europeans, they could stop fearing the imperialist Russians, who regarded them as their subjects. They also wanted to live like Europeans, because that sort of life seemed better, safer, more affluent, and carefree. Lara, too, dreamed of a life like that for her sons. But for the Georgians, it was a pipe dream, and in the gorge especially so. For Europe to hear them knocking at the door, first the Georgians had to get rid of the Chechen insurgents. So they were more likely to have a war ahead of them than to be transformed into Europeans. And it looked inevitable, because to protect themselves from a Russian invasion, the Georgians had invited soldiers from America to help them establish order in the Pankisi Gorge.

The insurgents were gearing up for war too. The Georgian president sent envoys to Pankisi to warn the insurgents that if they refused to leave of their own accord, the Georgians and Americans would have to force them out. The insurgent emir Gelayev agreed to leave the gorge, and as a way of thanking

Georgia for sheltering them, he promised that before taking his unit north across the mountains, he would travel west, to Abkhazia, to crush the local rebels, whom he had once supported in their uprising against the Georgians.

The Chechens needed guides to take them safely across the mountains. There were a hundred shepherds' and smugglers' trails leading across them. In all the Caucasus, nobody knew those trails better than the Kists, who lived among the mountains. Both Lara's brothers signed up to be guides for the insurgents. Her presence in the family home made it much easier for them to do this, because when their sisters married and left, the duty of caring for the house and for their parents had fallen on the brothers. If Lara hadn't returned, they couldn't both have gone with the insurgents—one of them would have had to stay at home. Free of responsibility for others, they prepared for the expedition, getting their horses, saddlebags, tents, sleeping bags, and provisions ready. Every day they went out at dawn and only came home for supper.

"Next time, I'm going with you," Shamil announced one day. He was fifteen and regarded himself as an adult.

"You bet!" Lara's brothers said, laughing.

As she listened to their conversation at the table, Lara realized that if she were to remain in the gorge with the children, she might not know if her older son, once of legal age, decided to enlist in the rebel force. And there'd be nothing she could do to stop him. She could see how drawn he was to the insurgents already, just like all the boys in the gorge. They trailed after them and copied their way of speaking, behaving, and dressing; the older ones even tried to grow beards. She remembered her father's words. "You won't even notice when your boys change entirely into insurgents, into Arabs. They'll be off to war before you know it, and you won't get them back until you have to send them to the next world. Only then will you see them again."

As she talked to me, I could tell that she was casting her mind back to the toughest moments in her life, to the most important choices she'd ever had to make, to a time when no decision, however hard she set her mind to it, could guarantee that she was doing the right thing. To a time when she had had to choose between bad and worse solutions.

"I'm not the type to give in easily, but at that point, I could see that life was going to slip out of my control, and there was nothing I could do about it." She sighed heavily at the memory of that sense of helplessness. "I felt sick inside, I felt as if all the strength were draining out of me. But they say that if you refuse to admit defeat, good luck will favor you. How can we fail to believe that?"

Just then, her husband got in touch—the first time she'd had news of him since the outbreak of war. He was in Ingushetia and sent news through a friend who was going to Georgia. He asked the friend to tell Lara that he had left Grozny when the street fighting reached the city center. He had spent a few months in a refugee camp in Ingushetia and then, via Belarus and Poland, had made his way to western Europe. He'd been living there for four years and had managed to settle in and find work—nothing major, but he couldn't complain. Recently, he had been back to the Caucasus to see what had happened to their apartment and to his parents' house. And to visit their grave. Though they hadn't survived the war, they weren't killed by bullets or bombs; surprisingly, both had died natural deaths. There was nothing left of the apartment where he and Lara had lived in Grozny. Not just the apartment—nothing was still standing at all: none of the tower blocks, none of the houses that used to surround Minutka. There was just a vast heap of rubble—you couldn't tell what had once been where. There was nothing to go back to.

He had asked the friend to tell Lara that it would take him another week or two to sort out his affairs, and then he'd be leaving for Europe with the entire family, about fifty people. And that he'd like to take his sons with him—if, of course, Lara had no objection. In the country where he was now living, they'd have a better life and a better future. Undoubtedly better than in the Caucasus, where wars kept erupting, as if one sparked off another, with no end in sight. He didn't ask if Lara wanted go to Europe with him, nor did he suggest it. She understood. Anyway, she couldn't leave the gorge. She had to stay there to care for her aging parents, who couldn't be abandoned. And they would never have agreed to leave home for anything.

She agreed to hand the children over without hesitation. After all, she was entrusting them to their father, not a stranger. It didn't occur to her to ask the boys if they wanted to go. She and her husband arranged for another friend of his, who was on a business trip to Georgia, to drive the boys to Ingushetia; he'd stop in Jokolo to collect them on his way back. Their father would see to everything else, all the formalities and costs. He promised to call Lara as soon as they reached their new home in Europe.

"I was told that in Europe everyone sympathized with the Chechens and wanted to help. Apparently, anyone who arrived in Europe was given a European passport and a clean apartment, and their children could go to school—all free of charge."

Hearing these stories, Lara began to wonder if she'd done the right thing by taking the children to the Pankisi Gorge. Perhaps she should have stopped at a refugee camp in Ingushetia, at least for a while, and explored the opportunities for traveling to Western Europe. But at the time, her family home had seemed the safest place for them on earth.

"More coffee?" said a voice beside us. Lara jumped, knocking over her empty cardboard tea cup. There was a young man in a McDonald's uniform and cap standing at our table.

"I gave you a shock," he said apologetically. "I'm asking because the coffee's still free for the next five minutes, but then breakfast time will be over."

The young man was confused by our silence. Lara gazed at him absently, blinking. She didn't pick up the overturned cup; perhaps she hadn't noticed it rolling toward the edge of the table, or maybe it didn't bother her.

"Which means we're about to start serving from the main menu," the young man said. "Burgers . . . lots of customers come for the burgers," he went on, growing more uneasy. "May I take that cup now?"

Lara blinked as if she couldn't understand what he was saying. She asked for another cup of tea.

"Why not order it with a set meal?" the young man prompted. "It works out much cheaper."

She refused, so he hesitantly walked away. Maybe he was curious to know why we'd been sitting there for several hours, although he shouldn't have been surprised, because that wasn't unusual in McDonald's—lots of people came in, sat down, and stayed there all day.

Lara straightened her headscarf, a gesture that seemed to restore her sense of reality. But I couldn't help wondering where the real world was for her now.

"Sometimes I try to decide if a good mother should place her children in someone else's care. Even if it's their own father. But I wanted a better life for them, and it didn't look as if they could expect that in the gorge." She straightened her headscarf again. "Everyone wants the best for their children, don't they? In Pankisi, we copied the Georgians because we thought of them as superior to us. We drank wine with them because if they did it, it must have been integral to achieving a better life. And I decided to make my sons into Europeans."

As the clock struck noon, the restaurant began to fill up. A boy sat down at the table next to ours, the last one to be taken. He looked like a student. He opened a laptop and stirred sugar into his coffee in its cardboard cup.

"I wanted them to live in a world that's clean and nice, where people are polite to each other, nothing's in short supply, and whatever you order is brought to you at once. Just like here," she said, glancing around the restaurant.

A girl's face appeared on the computer screen at the next table. The boy put buds into his ears, then stared at the monitor and began to speak. Lost in thought, Lara gazed at him for a long while.

"That's how we used to talk, the children and I," she said, sighing. "Who'd have imagined it would end this way . . . I don't know," she said. "I thought I was doing the right thing, but look how it ended . . ."

It wasn't really an answer to my question; I had asked if her sons had settled in their new home and if they'd found it hard to adapt from Caucasian to European life. They must have felt lost, having to change their ways again, getting used to new places, new people, and a new pace of life. And having to learn a new language to understand what was going on around them.

"If I could turn back the clock, would I do anything differently?" Lara said, as if she hadn't heard the question. "Probably not. There was no alternative. Here they'd just have gone to waste."

She wasn't in any doubt as she said good-bye to her sons, making them hurry up and get in the car that was to take them to their father. She wanted them to be gone, the sooner the better, so she wouldn't have time to give in to despair.

She was calm, sure of her decision, even when news reached the gorge that Gelayev's insurgents who had gone to fight in Abkhazia had been defeated. Apparently, they'd planned a surprise action to capture the Abkhaz capital, Sukhumi, and also the city of Sochi, just across the border in Russia; then they were going to blackmail the Kremlin into agreeing to a ceasefire and withdrawing their troops from Chechnya. And if they failed to capture either city, they'd cross into Chechnya from Abkhazia, over the mountains that were home to the Kabardians and Circassians. They had chosen this longer, indirect route, through the Georgian provinces of Racha and Svaneti, because they were expecting the Russians to be lying in wait for them on the shorter route that led straight across the mountains. But the Russians were also waiting for the insurgents at the entrance to the Kodori Gorge, where they had planned to come down the mountains and slip through to Sukhumi. In fighting that continued for several days on the banks of the Kodori River, Gelayev lost so many men that he ordered a retreat. The insurgents tried to break through the siege to reach a pass leading to higher terrain, where they could evade pursuit. But very few managed to break out of the trap. There, on a mountainside above the Kodori, both Lara's brothers were killed. The insurgents buried them in a mass grave in the forest with all their fallen men, because they couldn't carry corpses across the mountains. They marked the burial site well, so the relatives would be able to transfer the remains to their own cemeteries at home.

The news about Lara's brothers was brought by Omar. He had recovered from his wounds and was well again, though he hadn't been fit enough to go with Gelayev's unit and had stayed behind. He didn't need looking after anymore, and Lara had stopped visiting his makeshift room on the porch. Since he'd been feeling stronger, he had spent less time in there anyway—he went out in the morning and came back at night, without wanting any supper. She didn't ask what he did all day or with whom he met; that was none of her business. She figured he met up with the other convalescent insurgents Gelayev had left behind in the gorge. They couldn't join his expedition, but they were still in touch with their comrades who had gone on it.

"I have bad news," he said. That day, he had come back later than usual. "Your brothers have been killed. Both of them."

Lara said nothing. She didn't even ask if he was sure. She leaned against the kitchen table as sudden, acute pain drained her strength away.

"It has been confirmed," added Omar.

On his way to the porch, he turned and said, "You were right to send your sons away from here."

"Thank you," she replied, probably too softly for him to hear.

She didn't need confirmation of this piece of news. As soon as her brothers announced at supper that they were going with Gelayev to guide the insurgents across the mountains, she had sensed that this would happen. Something instantly told her that if they joined the expedition, they'd never come home. It seemed inevitable.

When Omar told her they'd been killed, she felt pain, but also the sense of calm that comes when something that's bound to happen finally does, the feeling that her worst, irrational fears had been confirmed and that she hadn't been mistaken. So maybe she hadn't been wrong to send her sons to Europe, either.

"Surely it was tough for them, at least to begin with?" I asked. "That's a pretty big leap. One day the Caucasus, the next day the Alps."

Lara smoothed the edge of her headscarf.

"When my brothers were killed, I sensed the same thing would have happened to my boys. Omar said I'd done the right thing."

She didn't know how to tell her parents about her brothers'

death. How was she going to tell her mother she'd lost both sons? How could she tell her father? She felt her anger rising. Losing one child was an unbearable misfortune, but why did they both have to die? She wondered whether to wait until Gelayev's unit returned to the gorge, when everything would be explained. But before she could make a decision, her parents had learned the whole truth. Her mother wept in the kitchen, while her father shut himself in his room, refusing to speak to anyone.

None of the returning insurgents could say how Lara's brothers had died. None of the survivors had been near enough to witness their deaths. One of the local Kists who had joined the unit did confirm that he recognized their bodies. He also knew exactly where they'd been buried and was sure he'd be able to find the site, should the need arise.

"So I tell myself I did the right thing," Lara said again. "I couldn't go to Europe, even less so after my brothers' death. But I hadn't said goodbye to my sons forever. I thought they were just going away for a while and would be back when things calmed down. Anyway, it wasn't about me. I was only thinking of their best interests. And if life turned out to be better for them there, I could only be pleased that they were happy, and I'd be reconciled to the separation. I'd have gone to visit them, I'd have helped them at home and enjoyed being with my grandchildren. And they'd have known that as long as I was alive, they'd always have a home here too."

Her doubts left her when the elders finally managed to persuade the insurgents to get out of the gorge for good. "The Georgians say both Russia and America are putting pressure on them and that if they don't come fight us with one, they'll do it with the other, because they won't have any alternative," the old men explained. "We helped you as brothers when you were in need. Now you can help us if you don't want our destruction. If they bring us war, we'll lose our villages and our houses, which won't be a refuge for you anymore, either."

Gelayev had to go back into the mountains anyway, especially after the failure of his expedition to the Kodori Gorge. His old comrades in arms, as well as his rivals, had long since been reproaching him for letting his men grow idle in the Georgian valley instead of fighting the Russians; they said his inactive army was going to seed and that he'd lost his fighting spirit and wasn't the fearless warrior he used to be.

To avoid harming his hosts and benefactors, and also to regain his reputation, Gelayev assembled his unit and led them into the mountains. He was never seen in the gorge again, though he left a new wife there and the two sons she had borne him. He had left his first wife in Siberia, where he lived for many years before the war. She hadn't joined him when he decided to return to the Caucasus. His second wife was from the Pankisi Gorge, for which reason his Kist admirers had come to regard him as their brother and leader.

Before heading into the mountains, he sent his oldest son, Rustam, abroad. The boy had run away from his Russian mother to live with his father in the Caucasus and to fight in his unit. But now, as he set out to war, Gelayev sent Rustam to study at a Muslim academy in Cairo. Lara was planning to tell her sons about it if they didn't like living in Europe and were upset with her for sending them away from home. "Rustam, your school friend, has gone abroad too," she would say. "Since the emir sent him there, just as I've sent you to Europe, it must have been necessary."

Soon after the insurgents left the gorge, the Chechen refugees were gone too. Many of them decided to go back across the mountains, to Chechnya. "War or not, a person should be in his homeland, that's his place," they said. But the insurgents, who by taking up arms had cut off their own way back, sang a different tune. "Wherever we are, that's our home." Lara had often heard them say this, but it always felt as if they didn't actually believe it and were simply trying to disguise their own failure.

The Chechens who had decided to abandon the Caucasus and go abroad must have been thinking the same way. They'd gone to Europe and America, Turkey, Syria, Jordan, and Egypt. A hundred years earlier, the Chechens' neighbors the Circassians had set off on a similar migration. They had rebelled against Russia too, and it had crushed their insurgency just as cruelly, leaving them the choice of exile or slavery. The Circassians who sailed across the Black Sea to Turkey must have said goodbye to their cousins and neighbors in the same way as the Chechens setting out in all directions from the Pankisi Gorge. They exchanged wishes for a speedy reunion, but in their hearts, they knew they were leaving for good and that their paths would never cross again. So many of the Circassians had gone away that only a handful were left in the Caucasus; living like Russians in Russia, they gradually came to be just like them. The same thing happened to those who decided to go abroad. The ones who settled in Europe became like

Europeans, and the ones who chose to live in Turkey or in the Middle East became Turks and Arabs.

Lara believed that in her sons' case, wherever fate cast them ashore, they'd find a good new home, but they'd never forget the old one where they grew up, which would always be there for them. She also hoped that life among foreigners wouldn't change them as much as it had the Circassians, and that she wouldn't stop understanding them or become foreign to them.

Once the Chechens had left, the Pankisi Gorge felt deserted, as if there were no people in it. The long-forgotten peace and quiet returned to the villages, and the silence that suddenly fell was so profound that you could almost hear the trees rustling on the mountain slopes in the distance. Like bonfire smoke dispersed by the wind, the sense of anxiety disappeared; life calmed down and returned to its old flow—like the Alazani River, which always broke its banks in spring and cascaded into the Khaketian valleys with an ominous roar, but that, once rid of its surplus water, meandered along at its usual gentle pace.

Thanks to the sudden departure of the Chechens, and thanks mainly to the calm that now reigned in the gorge, as Lara waited for news from her sons, she was gripped by new quandaries.

"There had never been anything for the young people to do here, they had no occupation and no future. Nothing ever happened here. Some people don't mind that, or else they're like me—they enjoy the peace and quiet and don't feel that time is slipping through their fingers. But young men don't like it, they don't account for time, they still think they have more than enough of it. You can't shut them off from the world. They need ambitions, space, air. You can't take that away from them—why should they have to know at once that nothing major or important is likely to happen in their lives and that they might not come to anything special? They won't do any better than their parents and grandparents, but you can't say that to young people—it's better for them to find out for themselves."

She knew she had to be patient, because many days, maybe weeks, would go by before her sons reached their destination and made themselves at home in Europe. But she never imagined she'd have to wait five years, almost two thousand days.

At first, the lack of news didn't worry her. Lara thought of Europe as a safe oasis—you only had to get there to be free from all your troubles. She wasn't afraid of something bad happening to her sons there, just that they wouldn't be let in. She had heard rumors that in spite of the Chechens' stories of how welcome they were made to feel in the European capitals, more and more often, on arriving at the border, they were being sent back to where they came from. And those lucky enough to get across it were not being invited to live in brand-new, colorful houses and apartments built specially for them, but were sent to transit camps, where they lived under guard in barracks resembling prisons. There they were put through grueling interviews designed to determine if they deserved to become Europeans, or were criminals and subversives wanting to get into Europe with the sole aim of destroying it. Lara couldn't understand how anyone could want to ruin something that was said to be near perfection. She understood the need to vet everyone, to make sure there weren't any madmen hiding among the new arrivals, seized with the desire to destroy born of hatred or envy.

Her only concern was that a mistake could be made during the screening process, at her sons' cost—what if they were regarded as unworthy of Europe or, God forbid, as its enemies? That was her only real fear.

The stone fell from her heart when she heard that they had been allowed across the border and were now somewhere in Europe. She learned this from relatives of her husband's in Ingushetia. They had been on the point of leaving too, and to gather advance information and advice, they'd been making an effort to keep in touch with earlier migrants, who passed on news through friends and chance acquaintances, and occasional phone calls. Through mutual acquaintances, they told Lara the news that her husband and sons had arrived in the Alps and were safe and well.

Lara had no idea how to look for them; she didn't have their address or phone number. She had no device they could call her on. And when she finally saved up enough to buy a new, pocket-size cell phone, she had no way of telling her sons about it. All she could do was wait to hear from them, while mentally composing their first conversation.

Until, one day, at the marketplace in Duisi, an unfamiliar boy stopped her and said he'd spoken to Shamil the day before. Lara was stunned. The boy said he and Shamil had been friends for ages—they'd been at the same school, and they'd studied Arabic together at the new mosque. Recently, they'd reconnected via the Internet. At first they'd just corresponded by email, but last week, on Shamil's advice, he'd installed a tiny camera on his computer, and for the past two evenings they'd not only chatted, but had seen each other on their computer screens. Yesterday, Shamil had asked the boy to find his mother and tell her he'd like to talk to her that way too. The boy said that if Lara had a computer at home, she only had to install the right program and buy a small camera in Telavi. He promised to help her do this.

Lara didn't have a computer at home. She didn't need one, nor could she afford such a luxury. The boy offered to come to her house that evening and contact her son using his own computer. She said, "No, thank you"—she didn't want to talk to her sons in the presence of a stranger, at least not for the first time after five years' separation.

"This is his address," the boy said, taking a piece of paper from his pocket with a string of letters neatly written out on it. "He asked me to give it to you. You only have to hook up the camera, enter the address, and you'll be able to talk. As if you were sitting at the same table, facing each other. The only thing you can't do is touch."

Though she still had some matters to settle at the local administration in Duisi, Lara finished her shopping at the market and went straight back to Jokolo, where she immediately started asking who in the village had a computer. Two of the farmhouses had them, one of which was nearby. The owners agreed for her to drop in that evening and use their computer to talk to her sons. Seeing the helpless look on her face, their teenage daughter promised to show her how it worked and to give her whatever help she needed.

It was dark by the time she left the house to hear and see her sons for the first time in five years. Shamil was twenty by now. The last time she'd seen him, he was a proud, rebellious teenager. Now he was a grown man. And Rashid! When he left, he was a child. Would she recognize him as a seventeen-year-old?

The girl sat her down at the computer and typed out the magic spell that would summon up Lara's sons.

"When they appear on the screen, just speak," she said, and left the room, closing the door behind her. "And you can talk for as long as you like. It doesn't cost a penny."

Lara sat staring at the colorful screen. Her head was roaring and her mind was full of confusion. Her heart was racing, she felt breathless, as if the next wave of heat flooding her body would stifle her. "Shamil, aged twenty; Rashid, aged seventeen. Shamil, aged twenty," she kept repeating, staring at the button on the keyboard she was to press when her sons answered from the other end. She knew Shamil would be the first. "Shamil, aged twenty, a grown man . . ."

She was torn between excitement and fear of what was about to happen. She couldn't wait to see her sons' faces on the screen and to start talking to them, but she also felt overwhelmed by insecurity, afraid she wasn't ready for this encounter and that it was all happening too quickly. If the connection had broken off at that moment, she'd have run home in relief, promising herself she'd come back tomorrow, feeling braver and knowing what to say.

She'd been waiting for eight minutes when the face of a bearded man appeared on the screen, smiling at her hesitantly.

"Mom, are you there?" she heard. "Do you recognize me? It's me, Shamil."

She couldn't hold back her tears.

"Mom? Are you crying? We're doing really well. How are you? Rashid's here too. Can you see him?"

That evening, though they were together for more than an hour and a half, they spent more time looking at each other than talking. And what could she ask first, when so much had happened and so much had changed?

"My God! Is that really you? You're so grown up! I'd have walked past my own sons in the street without recognizing you."

"You haven't changed at all. It's as if a week had gone by, not five years."

As they gazed at each other, they felt emotional but awkward too, embarrassed by the lack of familiarity that had grown between them. But with every minute, with every word, they were getting used to each other again, and though at first stiff, the conversation soon began to take off. Typically, Shamil did his best to maintain polite indifference and not show his feelings or betray the fact that he'd missed her. But from his voice, she could tell how very excited and pleased he was to see her. Rashid didn't hide his delight at all.

"We had to learn another new language because everyone here speaks German, and we couldn't understand a thing." He poured out the words as if afraid he wouldn't have time to say everything that mattered.

"You couldn't understand Georgian at first either, but you learned it," she said.

"It was really hard," he replied.

"Arabic's even harder, but you learned that."

Shamil in particular had always amazed everyone with his ability to learn foreign languages, his sense of their basics as well as their special features. He only had to spend time in the presence of a foreigner to be able to copy him extremely well. "He'll grow up to be a musician," his teachers at the school in Grozny had predicted. It had only taken him a few months to master Arabic by attending prayers and lessons at the mosque in Duisi. As a reward, the imam had given him a copy of the Koran, which he used to read aloud at home in the evenings, learning the surahs by heart. "Do you want to be a mullah?" Lara's brothers had teased him, and the boy would solemnly reply that it was the duty of every Muslim to know the word of God as revealed to the Prophet. And they should know it just as it was recorded, in Arabic, for any attempt to translate it was iconoclastic sacrilege.

By now he knew half a dozen languages. When he left the gorge, he already spoke Chechen, Georgian, Russian, and Arabic. In Europe he had learned German, French, and Turkish, and was just starting on English. He wanted to see the world, and simply being able to communicate in a foreign language gave him the illusion of travel or of impersonating others. Lara thought he'd inherited this tendency to play roles from her. He saw languages as part of his future, though he didn't know what profession they might help him enter. He regarded the job he had now, working for a mail-order company, as just a temporary way of earning a living. He was considering studying linguistics. Whereas Rashid's passion was computers. He'd finished middle school and was already working part time at a computer store selling hardware and software.

The two were thrilled by Europe—her worries had been in vain. "It's like paradise here!" they both agreed. "They've got everything you could possibly want, you just have to go to the store. You can go in the middle of the night if you like, because they never close. And you don't even have to go there—you can order something and they bring it to your house. Like in a fairy tale. If you want something, you just snap your fingers and it's there! You can do what you like, say what you like, and no one can stop you. No holds barred, life is for living!"

Shamil took out his wallet and showed her a passport with a dark-red cover. He pointed at a row of gold letters.

"It says here that we're citizens of Europe," he said. "Dad has one too, and Rashid'll get his next year, when he's eighteen. If you came here and decided to stay, they'd give you one too. They have rules here that families have to be together, so they give you a passport without making a fuss."

They had become Europeans in Poland, where, after a stay in a transit camp, they'd been issued their new travel documents. Then they had traveled on to the Alps, to join their father, who already had a European passport and had gone on ahead. They realized that instead of waiting with them in Poland, where he wasn't earning any money, he would do better to go home, and then his sons and cousins would join him as soon as they had their European passports.

Lara's husband already had his own apartment and a job in a small town in the Alps. Both had been provided by the local authorities. He worked nights at a bus depot, cleaning and washing the vehicles to be ready to go out on the road again at dawn. By day he earned some extra cash at a Turkish restaurant a few blocks from where he lived, preparing the meat for shish kebabs. Since his sons' arrival, he had also been working at a nearby fruit and vegetable store run by an Egyptian acquaintance. He spent almost all his time at work, came home at dawn to sleep a few hours, and then went out again before noon. Friends and neighbors kept telling him to slow down or he'd work himself to death—why do that to himself? He'd reply that he hadn't brought his sons to Europe just to stare at it like a storefront window without being able to go inside and take advantage of everything on offer. "In that situation, not just young people, but adults, too, get so furious that they only have to pick up a stone and, without a second thought, they'll smash it all to pieces," he'd say. "I'd rather they had money than had to steal. Why work your fingers to the bone if not to make life easier for your children?"

Working such long hours, he hardly saw his sons at all, but thanks to the money he earned, they could afford things that other people couldn't. He was able to buy the boys the same clothes, shoes, and cell phones the other kids at their European school had. He wanted to make sure they weren't inferior to them in any way.

They didn't have to pay for the school, and the rent charged by the housing authority wasn't high. They could have moved and bought an apartment in another, better district, but they figured things were fine as they were. Almost everyone in their neighborhood was Chechen. The local authorities encouraged new arrivals to settle in this area, among their compatriots, assuming this would make it less difficult for them to adapt to their new life. And they were drawn to their own kind anyway, because it was easier to find a home, a job, and some support among friends. When Lara's husband went to work, he left his sons in the care of his female cousins or neighbors and didn't have to worry about them drifting around without supervision.

Years later, when Lara went to the town where they lived, she couldn't get over her amazement that it was more like the Caucasus than Europe.

"Everyone in the street and in the stores spoke Chechen," she said. "Whenever I went outside, it was like being in the marketplace in Grozny."

Their "Little Chechnya" was next door to a "Little Syria." Two blocks away there was "Little Kurdistan"—the Chechen boys had backyard fights with the Kurdish boys. And there were Turks living all around them. The western European locals rarely looked in here, regarding districts occupied by migrants as unsafe.

Lara was surprised by the large number of mosques too. There was one on every corner—one for Shi'ites, another for Sunnis, another for Sufis, another for Salafis—calling for the healing of Muslim souls through a return to the very roots of the faith and strict observance of all the rules recorded in the Koran. Lara felt as if she were constantly hearing the call to prayer coming from the minarets.

Her sons sided with the Salafis, who were like the imams from the new mosque in Duisi. They went to their mosque to pray and to study Arabic, and that was where they met their friends and acquaintances, spent their free time, and practiced hand-to-hand combat and weightlifting, just as the insurgents in the gorge had.

Their father had nothing against it; like Lara, he didn't think it posed a risk. He didn't have time to deal with his sons' spiritual education. In fact, he encouraged them to go to the mosque, to discover the faith of their forebears and learn how to live righteously. What could be wrong with that? "It's the one thing Europe won't give you," he'd stress. "They say God is dead, they don't need him anymore." He promised that one day, when things had settled down, he'd take them to the Caucasus and show them the mosques and the *aul* their family came from.

"Did you know that Rustam has gone abroad too?" Lara said, interrupting her son's account.

"Who's that?" Shamil asked in surprise.

"Rustam, Gelayev's son. His father sent him to Cairo."

"Yes, I know." Shamil didn't seem interested in this piece of information. "Cairo . . . It's better here, at our place . . ."

Lara was thrilled to have news of her sons and to hear Shamil speaking of his new home in Europe as "our place."

"Guess what—I got married," Shamil said. "Next time we talk, I'll bring my wife and introduce you."

Kheda was a Chechen girl of eighteen. Shamil had met her in Europe, but they had married in Caucasian style, observing the old customs. Only Lara, his mother, hadn't been at the wedding or the party, where the entire street had spent three days celebrating.

"We're expecting a child," Shamil said. "In three months' time, you're going to be a grandmother."

Lara could sense the anxiety clumsily hidden behind his outward nonchalance. He'd kept this news until the end of their conversation, once they'd fixed a time to talk again and Lara had given the boys her phone number.

"It'll all be okay," she said. "Everything's going to be fine now."

For his first-born son, Shamil had chosen the name Mohammed. Not a Chechen or a Caucasian name, but an Islamic one. This was his way of honoring the Prophet, the blessings and peace of Allah be upon Him, and of showing his son the path to the Almighty from the very start.

After this first conversation, they were often in touch on the phone or the computer. Lara borrowed some money from her neighbors to buy a secondhand laptop in Telavi, which she set up on a small table by her bed. Her sons usually called in the evening, which meant late at night in the Pankisi Gorge because of the time difference.

She talked to Shamil more often than with Rashid and soon noticed that he wound Arabic words into his speech, usually phrases from the Koran, which he knew by heart. One day, instead of greeting her, he mumbled, *Bismillah ir-Rahman-ir-Rahim*, "in the name of Allah, the Most Gracious, the Most Merciful." At the time, she laughed and said he shouldn't pray to her because it was a sin. Embarrassed, he explained that he'd just come home from the mosque.

He talked more and more often about the Koran, his faith, the mosque, and the people he had met there. She couldn't understand his religious zeal, but she couldn't see any harm in it either. One time she asked if he had any close friends, seeing he spent all his time at the mosque. He replied that he saw his close friends right there, at the mosque.

"What about Europeans?" she asked. "You must have some friends among them, surely?"

He said it was hard to make friends in Europe because no

one had the time. They worked from dawn till dusk—they'd probably work nonstop if they could, in the first place to prove their superiority and then to fight off their rivals.

"That's all that counts here, how much you've got and who you are in the rat race, so everyone tries their level best to acquire as much as possible. They never stop competing with each other." He said it angrily, which she found surprising and also rather alarming. "That's the only way they rate you here. If you own things, you're someone; they respect and admire you, and what you say matters. But if you have nothing, you're a nobody, and no one cares what you think."

He hung out almost exclusively with Chechens, and also Turks and Syrians from the neighborhood. He only had one good friend among the Europeans. They had met at school. Niko was a Croat, but his family had settled here a very long time ago. He'd been born in the Alps and was regarded as a native by the locals, who didn't count people like Shamil, migrants from far away with a different skin color and a different faith, as compatriots. A European passport like the one Shamil had been given was just a form of charity, a permit to enter their world, but it didn't entitle you to any familiarity or admit you to local society.

Lara also noticed that the more she talked to Shamil, the closer they became; and the more accustomed they grew to their long-distance conversations, the less positively he spoke about Europe. He no longer enthused about the shopping malls bursting with marvelous products, ready to make every dream come true, where he and Rashid used to spend their time. Now his comments were disdainful. "That's just small change, the consolation prizes," he once said angrily. When she asked what prizes he meant, and why he needed consolation, he was annoyed. His words worried her—to her, his mother, they implied that her son wasn't happy. She reassured herself that it didn't have anything to do with his marriage—for a while, she'd been afraid there might be something wrong between him and Kheda, the girl she didn't know. But it wasn't that. Shamil spoke with increasing irritation about the mail-order company where he worked, packing items into cardboard boxes, wrapping them in company paper, and sealing them with tape. He earned a decent living and had everything he needed.

"So are you satisfied?" she asked, just to make sure, and he said yes, so she sighed with relief.

He'd dropped the idea of going to university, because he had to support his family and he didn't think it was right for a husband and father to be a student. He had signed up for some evening computer and accountancy courses. He said that higher qualifications would make it easier for him to get promoted and would secure him better wages. And above all, they'd give him the opportunities he and Rashid had been told so much about when they'd first arrived in Europe. *Nothing is impossible, hold on to your dreams, you can achieve anything if you really want to, you're the architect of your own fortune, you're the captain of the ship.* That's what he'd heard at every step, and he liked the sound of it. And that, he kept saying, was his main concern.

Now and then he still met up with Niko, the Croat. It was always Niko who called him. He'd studied journalism and was hoping to work for one of the newspapers or at a radio or television station. If he did become a reporter, he wanted to specialize in the Caucasus. He figured that would give him a chance of success, because hardly any of the country's journalists knew enough about the Caucasus to comment on it. Apart from plain curiosity and their mutual fondness, Niko's friendship with Shamil brought the Caucasus and its affairs closer to him.

In fact, Niko's dream was to write books, and he figured journalism would take him in the right direction. He had published a few stories in a literary journal, and the reviewers had praised his light touch, his feeling for the topic, and his distinctive style. They said he showed promise, but no one wanted to publish his books, and he couldn't get a job in journalism. So he went on writing while working for a friend's company, but was starting to suffocate—he said he felt like a slave, a machine, a pack animal. Instead of moving forward and achieving the wonderful life he wanted, he kept running into the same old wall. He felt as if he were banging his head against it, then as if he were punching it again and again without breaking through at all. The longer it went on, the more the ropes around his neck, arms, and legs tightened, disabling him. He was afraid the time would come when he'd stop battling and would simply give up. With each passing day he was becoming more painfully aware that life was slipping through his hands, while he was going nowhere, losing his sense of purpose and meaning. He wasn't doing what he wanted or fulfilling what he'd been promised. He was only doing what he had to, what was demanded of him.

"Why are you telling me about this Niko guy?" Lara interrupted Shamil when, instead of giving her a plain account of the last few days and weeks, once again he started complaining about how unfairly his friend had been treated. "He has his own mother to talk to—you tell me about yourself."

Her conversations with her sons became her chief source of joy, the entire meaning of her life. They gave her the courage that comes from knowing the right choice has been made. She could stop worrying and feeling guilty. Everything was fine. Now she could start to live in peace, just for herself.

Maybe that's why she ignored the notes of disappointment she heard in Shamil's words. Or perhaps she didn't want to hear them? She chose to regard his bitterness as part of the superior pose her son liked to adopt. But finally, she had to ask.

"Son, are you really all right there?"

She was prompted by his constant talk about unhappy people who'd failed and about the bitter disappointment you feel when forced to abandon your dreams.

Shamil wanted more than to spend the rest of his adult life packing and sending parcels for a reasonable wage. Armed with the certificates from the training courses he'd completed, he had asked his managers for an interview. They arranged a meeting, where he explained that he could do more and wanted them to give him a more responsible job. He stressed that he was interested in applying and developing his best skills, not just in making money.

When they asked what he was good at, he said he had an exceptional ear for foreign languages and was fluent in several, and that he was a quick learner. "That's of no use to us here," one of the managers said. Another one advised him to be happy with what he had and not to clutter his head with fantasies—

where he came from, people probably couldn't dream of living as he did. "If you don't like it here, you can always go home. Don't forget that I can find a dozen takers for your job," he added. "Such are the times."

Indeed, times had changed. When they first came to Europe, they were told it was indecently rich but aging, and in need of extra hands to work. Every year, the local population was shrinking because they didn't want to have too many children, and only in old age did they worry about who was going to work in support of their retirement. But now those days were over. It turned out they'd been living and enjoying themselves on credit and had even spent the money that was meant to be their children's and grandchildren's inheritance. Articles had been appearing in the press about an imminent crisis and the need to economize. But so many job-seeking foreigners had been let into the country that there wasn't enough work for everyone, not even the worst, lowest-paid kind. The opportunities for picking and choosing from among the chances of a lifetime had run out, and all that remained was to be happy with what was still there for the taking.

Another time, Shamil told her about a Chechen friend of his who, before the war, had worked as an engineer at a petrochemical plant in Grozny. He had had no luck finding employment in the West that matched his qualifications and ambitions. Finally, he'd been offered a job as a security guard. "But I'm an engineer. I have fifteen years' experience at a major petrochemical plant," he said. "You *were* an engineer," the man at the employment agency said. "But now, as far as I can see, you're perfect for a job as a night watchman."

"There's no future here," Shamil said when Lara asked him point-blank if he was happy. He was upset at being cast in a mediocre role for the rest of his career when his life had only just started, and even more annoyed that he was expected to accept it and be grateful. However hard he tried, there was nothing he could do about it,

"What are you saying?" Lara protested. "You can see for yourself what you've achieved. You've got a family, a house, a job. And your whole life before you . . ."

"In which I'll do nothing but wrap parcels for dispatch . . ."

"Plenty of people would love to swap places with you."

"You're talking like one of them."

Now when he told her about his life in Europe, he no longer used the phrase "at our place," but increasingly talked about "them"—meaning everyone he blamed for his disenchantment, lack of success, and unfulfilled dreams. He no longer felt he shared a community with "them," nor did he seek their acceptance. On the contrary, conscious of the fact that they'd never allow him to be part of their world, he had started to stay away from it; suddenly it seemed worthless and empty and had lost its power to seduce him with its wealth and glitter. It was like a parcel wrapped in shiny, brightly colored paper, but with nothing inside. He started talking about his childhood, the insurgents in the village, their stories about the war, and their campfires in forest clearings.

"But you said living there was like paradise," Lara said sadly, still clinging to that beautiful vision from the past as she felt the first pinpricks of fear. "One day you'll come here, to the gorge, then you'll see how bad things can be," she said in a cautionary, almost hostile tone, because he had gone silent.

"At least I'd be at home," he replied.

When he and his friend Niko met up in town to complain about life, sometimes Niko told Shamil that he envied him. "I can only escape to my apartment. But it's empty, there's no one there, just four walls," he'd say. "At least you've got somewhere to go. You've got your mosque."

Shamil was indeed spending more and more time there. Lara soon learned to recognize the days when her son had been to the mosque. If, during their evening conversation, he talked about himself, his home, his son, and his wife, if he was calm and didn't complain or lose his temper, she knew that that day he'd been to the Salafis. He would also wind more Arabic words and phrases from the Koran into his speech than usual.

He said going to the mosque was a great help, it made him feel calm, and after praying he felt purified. He was careful not to leave out any of the prayers a Muslim is obliged to say five times in the course of the day. He did his best to go to the mosque to pray with the other believers, and only prayed at work on the rare days when he couldn't take a break from his duties. He told Lara that at his firm, as at many others in Europe, the management set a special room aside for this purpose. There was an arrow painted on the floor, pointing toward Mecca, so they could pray in the right direction. "There are more and more of us here," he often said, and one time, in a derisive tone, he told her about the guesthouse he'd visited where a Bible and a Koran had been left on the bedside table.

"Don't they pray in Europe?" Lara asked.

"Apparently they only pray on Sundays, but even then, their churches are empty," he replied.

Whereas on Friday, the Islamic holy day, his mosque was always full of people. He spent almost all his free time there and went home in the evening, after the fourth prayer, recited at sunset. Only then did he take care of his family and his domestic affairs. And before going to bed, he slipped out of the house one more time to run to the mosque for the fifth and final prayer.

One day, he told Lara that the mosque was the only place where he knew who he really was and why he'd been born.

"What do you mean, son? How can you not know who you are?" she protested in alarm.

He replied that he knew who he wasn't, but had only discovered who he was at the mosque. He definitely wasn't a citizen of Europe, despite having its passport in his pocket.

"A person is whoever he regards himself to be," she said.

"And that's exactly what I didn't know," he replied.

At the mosque, he was told, or maybe he realized for himself, that in the first place he was a Muslim, regardless of where he was from, where fate had cast him up, whether he was rich or poor, black or white. None of that mattered because, first and foremost, he was a servant of God, and he must live according to His will. He only had to remember to observe the divine commandments and act accordingly, and his life would gain a purpose and a direction. All his doubts would disappear, and he'd find simple answers to every question.

He told Lara that he found peace at the mosque because there he met people like him, just as lost and disappointed, unable to see the future ahead of them, filled with a vague sense of anger.

"I'm not alone there, but surrounded by my brothers, who feel the same way I do," he told her. "We understand each other at once, we have the same desires and the same things are missing from our lives."

Lara had long been aware of Shamil's sense of yearning for something, but she didn't ask where it came from or what he was missing in life. She figured it was the usual sort of quandary a young man endures as he enters adulthood and is forced to abandon some of his dreams. "It'll pass, it'll be over soon," she told herself.

She was pleased when he boasted to her about the large number of friends he'd made.

"That's good," she said. "You shouldn't be alone. People need to stick together. When you're all on your own, negative thoughts can get to you more easily."

She thought that when Shamil spoke about his friends, he meant the people he saw at the mosque. So she was quite surprised when he mentioned a friend from Paris, a person he knew in Brussels, and another in Hanover. She took these people as proof that although her son did so much grumbling, he was in fact putting down roots and becoming more settled in his new place. She didn't know that Shamil had never actually met most of these people in the flesh, but had gotten to know them by surfing the internet. He didn't know their real names, it was enough for him that they felt the same way he did and longed for the same thing. He had found his fraternal souls. Lara had no idea about that, but even if she had known, she wouldn't have been able to understand that you could make friends that way and that this sort of contact could change people's lives.

Eight years. All that time they'd been away from the gorge. She'd never imagined eight years could pass so quickly and imperceptibly. What had she done with those eight years of her life? She'd spent them on nothing but waiting. Waiting for news of her sons and from her sons, waiting to talk to them. What else? As she sat at the airport on the day they were due to fly in from Europe, she looked at the people in the arrivals hall. How had they spent the past eight years? So much had happened. How could all those things have occurred as if behind her back, without affecting her?

Soon after the boys had left for Europe, there had been riots in Tbilisi, and the old president had been deposed. People said that if he hadn't gone voluntarily, there would have been another civil war. But he was old, he knew that war is not a game and must be avoided at any cost. Moreover, the people respected him, and he won himself even more esteem by stepping down without trying to cling to power. They'd complained about him while he was in charge, saying he'd let matters slip and couldn't cope, not even with his own ministers and officials, who were shamelessly stealing state funds and robbing the public in broad daylight. Apparently he was afraid of them and simply tried to please everyone, as long as they didn't get into fights or provoke a new war. As a result, there was no authority in the country, no justice, just a power vacuum, thievery, and rising poverty. But when he stepped down without making a fuss, people felt sorry for him. Especially as he'd been ousted by the people he had groomed to be his successors and who owed him everything.

The new president was picture perfect—tall, handsome, and young, though many thought him *too* young. He'd spent time abroad, studying at foreign universities, and was fluent in several languages. He also had a foreign wife. He was the ideal European. He got straight down to the task, and nobody could deny he was a hard worker. He was everywhere at once, eager to take care of everything in person. Later on, the successes and the admiration turned his head, but few people could have achieved as much as he did in such a short time.

Time and again he restored order, put a stop to the thieving, and fired the venal officials, judges, and policemen, giving those who had profited from theft and bribery a choice—either return all the money to the state or go straight to jail. The people were very pleased with the new president for establishing justice and for wanting life in Georgia to be like that in Europe.

He had old roads resurfaced and new ones built; he ordered the construction of bridges, airports, train stations, hospitals, schools, and universities; he had everything cleaned, tidied, and repainted to make it look brand-new. As in Europe. *And he's done it, without a doubt,* Lara thought as she scanned the modern airport made of glass and steel. She'd only ever seen one like it in Western movies on TV.

But his achievements made the young president's head swell, and he never stopped boasting of them, behaving as if he had all the answers. Surrounded by sycophants, he was finding it harder and harder to take criticism. And as he was always impetuous, no wonder the people weren't pleased.

The Kists and Chechens from the Pankisi Gorge had a mistrustful attitude toward the new president. They couldn't forget that at the start of his presidency, in a bid to curry favor with Russia, he had ordered the arrest and extradition of several Chechens hiding in Georgia. It was pointless, because Moscow would never forgive him for wanting to be closer to Europe, and now they were just waiting to bully him or get rid of him. They knew how to trap him, how to provoke him into a new war against the Ossetians, and then, as if coming to the aid of Ossetia, they invaded Georgia. Soon there were Russian tanks at the gates of Mtskheta, and if Europe hadn't intervened, they would have advanced on Tbilisi with nothing to stop them. The few Chechen refugees remaining in the Pankisi Gorge said it was their autonomy that had saved the Georgians. If Georgia hadn't been an independent country, but a Russian province, the Russians would have razed it, just as they had Chechnya. Nobody would have protested or interfered, because it would have been an internal matter for Russia. But a sovereign country can't be invaded at the drop of a hat without provoking global outrage. Otherwise, the Russian troops would have crossed the mountains in a flash and would now be standing at the Alazani River.

Although the war had ended and life in Tbilisi had returned to normal, the airport was glaringly empty. It had been closed when Russian planes appeared over the city, but had reopened after the Russians withdrew. But there weren't many visitors coming to Georgia from abroad, although the fall is better than the summer for vacations in the Caucasus and for hiking in the mountains. But the foreigners had been scared off by the recent war and clearly thought Georgia was still unsafe.

As she looked around the deserted airport, Lara thought perhaps it was the war that had prompted her sons to visit her,
to return after eight years to the place from which she'd sent
them away. They were worried, they'd been asking if she was in
any danger, and they wanted to come see for themselves what
things were like in the gorge. They did their best to help her,
sending money from Europe, one time for her to buy a cow,
and another time firewood, for instance. They kept urging her
to come live with them. But she couldn't go—she had to look
after her parents, who had no one else left now. How could she
leave them on their own?

Since her sons had left for Europe, Georgia had changed
beyond recognition. But in the Pankisi Gorge, everything had
stayed the same, except that first the insurgents had left, followed shortly by almost all the Chechen refugees. At once, it
had become a quieter place, and it felt more spacious too. After
the Chechens, the foreigners who had come to help them had
gone as well. And without them, money, goods, and gifts for
the refugees stopped flowing into the Kist villages from abroad,
items they used to sell at the marketplaces along the river.

The old, familiar poverty had returned to the gorge. With
its sights set on Europe, Georgia drove ahead blindly, seething
with energy, ambitions, major plans, and undertakings. The
effects could be felt even in Kakheti. But in Pankisi, life was at
a standstill. Nothing was happening; nothing was being built.
On rare occasions, usually before an election, officials and politicians came from the capital and made extravagant promises.
Then they left, but nothing ever changed. Georgia was trying
to catch up with Europe, but as ever, the only option for the

Kists to earn a few miserable pennies was to herd sheep on the highland pastures or gather chestnuts in the forest. The young people were leaving to find jobs abroad, nowadays in Turkey and the Middle East rather than in Russia. They gave each other support. Anyone who settled in Istanbul, Damascus, or Cairo told their relatives and neighbors about it, then helped them find work and a place to live too. They sent money home to the family members they'd left behind. Some of them did so well abroad that their relatives built large, grand houses in the villages.

The few foreigners who occasionally dropped in at Pankisi encouraged the Kists to try to live off tourists, as the Khevsurians from the next valley or the Svans were doing. There was no need to work their fingers to the bone, they only had to guide visitors along the trails through the mountain passes, give them a bed, food and wine, and sit around the bonfire at night telling them the old legends. Easy money would flow into their pockets for nothing but hospitality.

Lara had been giving this idea some serious thought. The large house was well suited to being a guesthouse. It was almost empty. An entire floor, four rooms, could be hired out to summer vacationers. She liked receiving visitors and hearing their stories from the world outside. Her cousin Ali knew every track through the mountains, every stream and stone. He had served as a guide for the insurgents, so he could guide tourists too. At night, they'd come back to rest at Lara's house, and she'd take them to the cultural center, where she and the other local women would sing the old Kist songs and recite the old legends. She wondered what her sons would think. If the business took off, they could run the guesthouse together, they could invite their friends from Europe to the mountains and bring in visitors. Maybe they'd even return to the gorge, with their families, and they'd be together again.

She was roused from her reverie by an announcement over the airport loudspeaker. The plane from Europe on which Shamil and Rashid were due to arrive had just landed. She stood facing the exit so she wouldn't miss the moment they appeared. For the first time in eight years she was going to touch and hug her own children. They were only coming for two weeks, but she'd decided not to worry about that, or she'd spoil her joy. After all, who knows what life will bring?

They were the first to emerge. Although she recognized them at once, they seemed strangely alien, not like her sons, but adult men about whose lives she knew so little. She burst into tears when they came up to embrace her. They hugged and comforted her, saying, "It's all right now," "No need to cry."

"It's nothing, I just . . ." she replied. "From happiness."

They stood there for a long while, alone in the empty arrivals hall. Even the cab drivers, who usually rushed toward arriving passengers to grab their luggage and hasten them to their cars, left them in peace.

"How quick you were," she said, wiping her tears with a handkerchief. "They haven't let anyone else out yet."

"That's because we didn't stand in the line for Georgians, but the one for EU citizens," Rashid said. "They send you through faster there. If you're from Europe, you don't need a visa, and they let you in at once."

"And there were hardly any foreigners on the plane. Only

about three people apart from us, so it was quick," Shamil added. "All the other passengers were Georgians."

"The Georgians want to be accepted into Europe, but we Chechens are already one hundred percent Europeans. Just look at this!" Rashid said, taking his passport out of his jacket pocket.

Lara took hold of it carefully, as if afraid of damaging it, this permit to a better life and a better world. It had a stiff dark-red cover, with words in a foreign language written on it in gold letters. But she recognized the word *Europe*. She opened the passport to look at the photo.

"How wonderful!" She sighed. "It makes you glad to be alive!"

She remembered those fourteen days spent with her sons in the gorge as a time when she gently soaked up the joy that had replaced her fear and insecurity. She told them about herself and what had been happening in their absence, about their relatives, neighbors, closer and more distant friends. But above all, she questioned them about their life in Europe and the Western world, which was so often discussed in Georgia, presented as the Promised Land, where everything was in abundance and no one had any cares or problems.

They'd sit on the porch, gazing at the river and the distant mountains; or in the kitchen, at a table under the window. She liked to watch them enjoying her freshly baked homemade treats, pancakes, smoked fish, salty *sulguni* cheese, honey, and the pickles she always made for the winter. Lara busied herself at the oven, clanking pots as she made them their favorite dishes for supper—thick *lobio* stew made with kidney beans, onion, herbs, nuts and garlic, and *khinkali* dumplings stuffed with lamb. With her back turned, she listened as they talked, drinking in the sound of their voices. Sometimes their conversation shifted into German, and Lara sensed they were doing it to hide something from her. But even then, she could feel herself bursting with pride and joy that her sons had grown up to be so well educated and familiar with the world. She also liked walking around the village with them; everyone they met stopped to greet them, and remembering the boys from the past, they were full of delight and admiration to see what fine young men they had grown up to be.

Shamil and Rashid also tried to find their old childhood friends, but not many were left. Some had joined the insurgents and been killed in the mountains in skirmishes with Russian patrols. Most had gone away in search of work, to Europe, Turkey, and the Middle East. A small number had gone there to study. And the ones who had stayed behind were desperate to leave, to break free from the stagnation and hopelessness prevailing in the gorge; they spent their time by the river, getting high on wine and *anasha*, the local name for the plant known as Indian hemp. They urged Lara's sons to join them, but they flatly refused, especially Shamil.

"It's not right for a good Muslim," he said. "It's a sin, it's *haram*."

But they did go and spend time at the new mosque in Duisi, though they didn't find many of their old friends there either.

During their visit, Lara didn't like the fact that they were spending so much time at the new mosque. "Did you come to see them or me?" she asked, as if joking. Nor did she like it when Shamil talked at the table about politics, the state of the world, and about wars while complaining about the injustices and harm inflicted on Muslims. And she didn't like it when he talked about Islam, how a good Muslim should live and what he wasn't allowed to do. In Lara's view, too many things were forbidden according to her son, just about everything that gave people joy. She couldn't understand why he wanted to take so many things away from people.

"I don't want to take away people's joy at all," he replied. "But they should rid themselves of everything that draws their minds toward evil and away from God."

He didn't approve of his mother taking part in the choir at the cultural center and singing songs that weren't in praise of Allah. He was even more shocked by his mother's friends from the dance group. In his opinion, dancing was lascivious behavior that led to temptation and should be banned entirely. With barely concealed reproach, he pointed out that despite professing the Muslim faith, the local women did not dress respectably, left the house without men to guard them, and didn't cover their hair and faces when outside.

"You'd shut women up indoors!" Lara told him one day at lunch. "You talk as if you want to go back to medieval times. But you live in Europe, amid progress! Aren't you ashamed? Nothing here pleases you, you find fault with everything."

"Momma, I don't want to argue with you," he replied. "But don't imagine Europe is all that wonderful. It's not paradise, you can't be sure of anything there, nothing's permanent. And progress is when people feel they're living better. But it doesn't just mean well-stocked stores, a bank account, and not being allowed to ban anything. People need more than that in their lives, they need law and order, consistency. They need to believe in something, to understand why they're here on earth. There's none of that in Europe, although there's plenty of everything else."

"If it were that bad in Europe, people wouldn't be pushing each other out of the way to get there," Lara said.

"But once they get there, they find out that in their new place they're nobody and no one respects them. Why should they deserve respect? They're nobody, and they're going to stay nobody forever."

She wanted to say that surely not everyone ended up like that—there must also be people who did well in their new location, who were happy with life and respected. She wanted to say that they themselves were an example. But Shamil wasn't listening anymore, his thoughts were far away, in a place where Lara was afraid to go.

"Everywhere our brothers and sisters are suffering exploitation and tyranny," he suddenly said. "In Palestine, Kashmir, Chechnya, Bosnia, Afghanistan, Iraq... Everywhere... They're all against us. But the time will come when, with God's help, *inshallah*, there will be peace, and order, and justice, and the true faith will reign in the world. We just have to stand up for our people, we must fight, not sit with our arms folded, grumbling like old women!"

Another time, they quarreled about the village elders who, since the Chechens had left, were running their own system of government in the gorge again. The argument was about a car crash that everyone in Pankisi was talking about. A young man from Duisi had run a woman over in the road. Her relatives had taken her to the hospital in Telavi, and the entire gorge was waiting to see if she'd survive, and if she did, whether she'd be disabled for the rest of her life. Worse yet, it turned out that before getting behind the wheel, the young man had been drinking heavily with his pals. But nobody had called the police station in Duisi or summoned the police to the site of the accident; customarily, the police didn't interfere in the Kists' business unless the Kists asked them to. And no self-respecting Kist would go complain to the police, knowing that by doing so he'd dishonor himself and his entire clan. So no one had called the police when the drunk driver ran the woman over, which meant that the elders would be taking care of the entire matter, in their own way. Shamil couldn't accept this. He was outraged that the boy's family would pay the victim compensation set by the elders, and the rogue would get off scot-free.

"They're not even taking away his driver's license. What if, a month from now, he gets drunk again and knocks someone else over? If he did his time in the slammer, he'd soon wise up."

"Have you ever heard of anyone coming out of prison a better person?" Lara replied. "What will the victim gain from that sort of punishment? Knowing that two people's lives will be ruined instead of just one?"

"This way, all you're doing is protecting criminals, nurturing serpents in your own bosom. But it's all there in the Koran— what should be done and how to do it, from start to finish. If there's a crime, there has to be a punishment for it too."

"Our elders know how to arbitrate quickly and fairly. And they don't have to be paid for it. What matters most is to live in peace and harmony, and not lose lives because of revenge."

Traditionally among the Caucasian highlanders, achieving justice through revenge was not a privilege but a requirement. The family of any murder victim had to apply to the council of elders for permission to take the killer's life. The wrongdoer and his family could also present their case to the council of elders, defend themselves, prove their innocence, swear on the Koran, or ask for a guarantee from compatriots with a spotless reputation. But the sentence the elders eventually handed down was final and indisputable. If they decided that a crime had been committed, and the culprit deserved to die, his only chance of survival was to run away. His relatives had no choice but to renounce him, give him up to the avengers, and ask the elders for the murderer's death and the destruction of his house to be adequate compensation for the blood he had shed, and for his closest relatives and descendants to be spared. But sometimes the murderer died before vengeance had been taken on him. Then nothing could be done, and his sons would have to answer for their father's dishonorable deeds, and quite often his grandsons too. The law of revenge, exacted against not just the perpetrator of a crime but his entire family, was meant to be a strong enough deterrent to protect people from being tempted to do any harm to others.

But even this strictest of highland laws had not proved harsh enough to overcome the weakness of human nature; over time, to stop the bloodshed, the Caucasian elders had started to introduce new customs. Their method was to calculate the value of death and injury in terms of cows or sheep and to determine the level of compensation for death, disability, or wounding accordingly. They also encouraged victims' families to agree to these payments instead of insisting on settling scores by killing the wrongdoers.

And so they estimated that a death could be redeemed for seventy head of cattle, and ten cows constituted an adequate fine for wounding someone with a dagger or a gun. Yet the harm caused by wounding a woman was priced at only a dozen sheep, three cows, or the equivalent of one and a half bulls, which among the Caucasian highlanders were worth almost twice as much as heifers. From the rate of the fines, it appeared that the elders regarded a man's life as three times more valuable than a woman's.

A payment of thirty cows was set as the penalty for blinding, twenty-five for depriving someone of their right hand, and twenty-two for their left. The penalty for knocking out a tooth was one cow, the same as for depriving someone of a little finger. But for a middle finger you had to pay three cows (the same as for wounding a woman), and for a thumb the price was as high as five.

The rate of the penalty for theft was seven times the value of the stolen items. The compensation could be paid in kind, in heads of cattle or sheep, in cash, or in barrels of honey, which served in the mountains not just as food and medicine for certain ailments, but also as a method of mummifying the bodies of those who died in the heat of summer.

Lara believed that paying compensation and offering forgiveness were better than revenge—anything, anything at all, was better than killing, and the suffering and despair that death left behind. "You must live! Live, not die," she said every time, on every occasion, over and over, sensing in advance that this truth, though obvious to her, wasn't getting through to others. She couldn't understand why they were deaf to it—why was it so hard for them to comprehend?

"For some that's peace, for others slavery," Shamil answered her. "Those who find it convenient and acceptable are happy with that forever. So none of them try to change anything, they never stop crying: 'Peace! Peace is what matters most!' But what are the people who don't find it acceptable going to say? For them, peace means only that nothing's ever going to change and that they're always going to be at the bottom, just as they are now. If that's peace, how can you be surprised they don't put it at the top of their priorities?"

"Stop it, I refuse to hear about war," she interrupted.

"Why?" he said, feigning surprise. "Fighting and giving up your life for your faith is the sacred duty of every Muslim. Just believing isn't enough for you to deserve salvation. That would be far too easy!"

He knew that every mention of war upset his mother. She couldn't bear to hear him talking about death and martyrdom. In the past she had protected her sons from war, but now she couldn't help thinking that perhaps it would have been better if they'd seen and experienced it for themselves. Then Shamil wouldn't be talking about it in such wistful tones. War can't seduce you if you've seen and lived through it. It only attracts people who don't know what it's really like.

"Don't talk to me about war," she said.

But Shamil wanted to talk about it. And he wanted to know how Gelayev had been killed, the Chechen commander who had lived in the gorge with the insurgents and had taken control. The Kists had admired him and seen him as a hero, a demigod. When he was killed, the whole gorge went into mourning as if one of its leading residents had died.

"I don't know anything about it," she said curtly, though it was on the expedition led by Gelayev that her brothers had been killed. "Go and ask Omar. Omar knows best."

As we talked at McDonald's, Lara rocked gently in her chair, a steady, monotonous motion. From the next room came the happy cries of children; someone was having a fifth birthday party. The pool of sunlight we'd been sitting in that morning had long since passed our table and moved on. Now it was the afternoon.

"Yes, yes," Lara said, almost dispassionately, with a sort of pained humility, as if accepting a fair sentence. "I sent them to Omar myself. They came for two weeks, and I sent them to him. But my thinking was that it might finally put them off war—they'd see what it can do to a man, how badly it can destroy him. Then they wouldn't imagine it was just heroism, martyrdom, and justice. Everything I did was designed to put them off war, but everything I did just pushed them toward it. It must have been their destiny, but why did I have to engineer it?"

Although he'd licked his wounds and escaped the jaws of death, Omar had never returned to the land of the living. They said in the gorge that although he was among them, he wasn't really with them; he'd been too close to the brink to come back entirely. It's impossible to cross the border between life and death and then go on living without paying a price for it.

He had moved out of Lara's house and gone back to his relatives in the neighboring village of Birkiani, where there was
room for him once the Chechen refugees moved out. But he
hadn't stayed there for long. He was altered somehow, absent,
as if nothing mattered to him. Human affairs had ceased to
interest him, he was indifferent to his neighbors' quarrels, troubles, and poverty, and to the injustice they faced from various
officials. But also to their joys. He didn't seem to care about
vengeance or forgiveness, war or peace. He had no opinion on
any of these things. In the past, he had expressed his views like
everyone else, but that was long ago, as if in a former incarnation. Now he had no urge to say what he thought about
anything at all. Except perhaps the weather—if it was the right
time to gather chestnuts or drive the cows and sheep from one
pasture to another. He responded to everything with the sort
of genial smile that adults bestow on ignorant children who
haven't had any experience of life yet. Sometimes he spoke
so quietly that the words had to be guessed, and sometimes
they were completely incomprehensible. Until finally one day
he went into the mountains, where he now lived on his own,
grazing the village herds of cows, sheep, and goats.

That was where I met him, at the herdsmen's camp that had
been his home ever since he'd turned his back on people. It was
October, the season for gathering chestnuts, the last task in the
fall. Once it was done, the Kists got ready for winter.

The herdsmen's camp was in a small clearing among some
hundred-year-old trees. Besides Omar, about a dozen families
were here to gather chestnuts in the woods. The chestnuts were
put into large, strong sacks, which every few days were taken

down to the gorge by horse or in the beds of the old trucks the villagers used for expeditions into the mountains to fell trees for firewood and fetch building materials they could sell.

The chestnut gatherers and herdsmen lived in tarpaulin tents and shacks. Omar, small, thin, and wiry, wearing an army jacket and soldier's boots, lived in his own cabin, which he'd built for himself in the forest. Some of the villagers had helped him, giving him whatever they had to spare in their farmyards that might come in handy—wooden boards, old doors and windows, panes of glass, and furniture. From the power plant on the river, they'd towed in a small shipping container that years ago had housed the workers renovating the dam. It served Omar as the skeleton for his home.

I was curious to set eyes on a man who has escaped the jaws of death and to see how it had changed him, but there was nothing unusual about Omar's appearance. Withdrawn, as if shy, he flashed his gold teeth in a smile. But the people who had come here to gather chestnuts, both the young and the old herdsmen, obeyed him, compliantly carrying out the orders he issued in a soft, barely audible voice. Here, he was the boss, in charge of everything.

Every two or three days he went up the mountain to a larger clearing, where he stood on a wind-toppled oak tree to catch a cell phone signal. He checked the messages on his voice mail, which were usually to do with the packhorses he sent from up the mountain to a river crossing point to collect equipment, food, clothing, and tools for the camp. His water came from mountain streams. Sometimes there were calls to Omar from the gorge to announce guests, foreign tourists visiting the gorge who wanted to stay the night among the herdsmen and listen to Omar's stories around the campfire.

In spring and summer, some of the young men from the gorge were sent to live at Omar's camp in the clearing, to help with the cows, sheep, and horses. They also made cheeses, and sheep's wool felt for blankets, rugs, warm clothing, and hats. Some of them stayed up in the mountains for months on end, while others swapped places after a few weeks. Apart from school and work at their small family farms, there was no other occupation for the young men in the gorge. Because he hosted them at his clearing, Omar knew most of the Kists from the villages along the river. The young men came to his camp not just to work, but also to get away from the control of the elders and to have a good time together by the campfire.

When the chestnut season ended, Omar was left alone in the mountains. If he could, he'd have lived there all winter, but he was driven down to the gorge by severe blizzards that could bury the forest roads in a layer of snow several yards deep. Then it was impossible to reach his clearing by horse or truck, and wading through the snowdrifts on foot was out of the question, so he'd come and live with his relatives in Birkiani, but as soon as the weather improved, he'd go back into the mountains.

I arrived at the herdsmen's camp at noon. Late. Quiet and shaded, the clearing seemed deserted. I noticed the herdsmen's shacks underneath the trees only once my eyes were used to the dirty, yellow foliage on the forest floor.

Toward evening, people started flocking to the camp, chestnut gatherers laden with bulging sacks and herdsmen rounding up barrel-shaped cows for the night. Along with them some large sheepdogs appeared; Omar kept a whole pack of them here to protect the herds from wolves and bears.

The women had lit the stoves and were busily making supper, urging the children to go drive the animals into a pen. The men came and sat outside Omar's house on logs set around a stone hearth. The younger ones went into the forest to fetch wood for the campfire.

Finally Omar appeared too. He sat down outside his house among the men and chopped some meat to make kebabs. He cut it into small pieces and speared them onto skewers whittled from twigs. Once the herdsmen had lit the campfire, Omar waved acrid smoke aside, positioned the skewers above the flames, and kept watch over the meat. Once he thought the kebabs were ready, he shared them among the men sitting in the circle. He raked aside some embers and threw whole handfuls of chestnuts into them.

"They're delicious when they're well roasted. Everything's good that does people good," he said, staring into the fire, and the herdsmen gathered around him exchanged inquiring glances, trying to guess whether Omar was just amusing the guest or starting one of his stories.

They cocked an ear, because there were profound truths in the tales he told by the campfire, answers to some vital questions, or clues about life that might be useful. They saw Omar as a sort of hermit and sage, someone who because of his own mixed fortunes and experiences had come close to things that ordinary people don't understand.

He was a man of few words. Sometimes he said nothing for days on end, but was far away, lost in thought. At those times, people said he must be remembering the road he'd traveled, from the world of the living to the dead and back again, and that he shouldn't be disturbed, or he might get lost and fail to find his way home.

After being wounded during the winter battle for Grozny, he had spent three days lying among the corpses in Minutka. The bullets had injured his spine and deprived him of the ability to move. He had lost consciousness, and when he regained it, he couldn't feel anything, not even pain. Nor could he cough out words or make any sound. He could hear everything around him, not clearly, but as if at a distance, muffled by a roaring noise. He hadn't lost his sight, but he couldn't move his head, so all he could see was what was in front of him.

He didn't immediately realize he was lying in a pile of corpses. The whole time it was dark, ranging from twilight to complete blackness. He figured he was in an enclosed space, a cellar perhaps. He could hear people's voices around him and the thunder of explosions and gunfire farther away. They brought something up and laid it next to him. At one point, he heard someone say that they couldn't wait any longer, but must start burying the dead. "The earth is frozen solid," someone else said. "We could light a fire to make it a bit softer. Or we could pull up the cellar floor with a crowbar and dig a pit there," the first voice replied. That was when Omar realized they'd assumed he was dead and were about to bury him with the corpses. They'd lay him in a pit dug in the cellar, toss corpses on top of him, and bury him alive. He felt a chill pass through him. It surprised him, because if he couldn't feel pain, where could that cold shiver have come from? Maybe it was the terror they say you feel just before death, when you know it's on its way and nothing can stop it, but you're not ready for it yet, you'd like to live a bit longer, you still have so many things to do. It occurred to him that he'd survive if he didn't close his eyes. The only way he could escape death was by catching someone's gaze and answering it with a stare. He was afraid he'd fall asleep and lose consciousness, then he'd be done for, there'd be no hope of rescue. To drive off his tiredness, he thought through every detail of his entire life, year after year.

Suddenly he was startled by a dazzling light. Just as abruptly as it had flashed on, it went out again. He despaired at the thought that he had fallen asleep and missed that one, crucial moment. But the light returned—it was shifting, now closer, now farther away, but it didn't go out. He realized that there were several sources of light. It looked as if it were coming from flashlights. He could hear voices, but he focused all his attention on the light, as if by sheer willpower he could force it to turn its beam on him. It flashed past close to him, almost sliding across his face, then vanishing, but it came straight back again. Now Omar could sense it, he knew it was stopping on his face. Dazzled by the brightness, he squinted, but then opened his eyes as wide as he could. Blinded, he couldn't see a thing, but he clearly heard someone say, "There's someone moving over here! This one's alive!"

They extracted him from the pile of corpses, carried him out of the city on a stretcher by night, and drove him to a hospital in Georgia. He knew he'd been rescued, and was going to survive. But he still couldn't move or feel anything, and the doctor said he might remain paralyzed for the rest of his life.

At first, he didn't believe it, but as each day passed without any improvement, he surrendered increasingly to doubt and stopped fighting. When he was on the point of giving up and was desperately praying for death, despite having previously escaped it, he regained the feeling in his right hand and started to move his fingers. The doctors gathered around him in amazement. "It's a miracle," they said, shaking their heads. "It's proof of how strongly he wanted to live."

And Omar recovered, regaining control of his body until, finally, the doctors agreed that he was back in the land of the living for good and didn't need them anymore. They told him to take care of himself and eat properly, and discharged him from the hospital. They asked if he had anywhere to go in the city, and when he said no, they advised him to go to the Pankisi Gorge, to join his own people. And that was how he had ended up at Lara's house.

He told himself that as soon as he gathered his strength, he'd join Gelayev's insurgent army. But before Omar was well enough for a journey across the mountains, Gelayev had set off for Abkhazia, where he was ambushed. Then Gelayev had made his way over the mountains to Ingushetia, where once again he was defeated by the Russians. Badly wounded, for a few months he had disappeared underground. Less than a year later, news went around the *auls* and valleys that he was recruiting a new unit, with the aim of breaking through to Chechnya and Dagestan, to go on fighting from there. Omar was pleased, because it looked as if Gelayev was planning to fight just across the border; he clearly wanted to have a safe base in Pankisi's Kist villages, a hideout for the winter. So Omar looked forward to the moment when the insurgents would come down to the gorge. He wanted to join them, and now he was ready.

But Gelayev didn't return to the gorge. In the middle of winter, he battled across the mountains with a small unit and, following the expedition to Chechnya, came back into Dagestan. Apparently from there he was planning to cross to the Georgian side and come to Pankisi, but he was ambushed by Russian troops. The insurgents scattered, but had no chance of escaping the manhunt that followed. Gelayev was killed fighting alone in the mountains.

"Someone must have given him away. There's always a traitor," Omar said when the conversation by the campfire turned to the insurgent commanders with whom I was familiar as a journalist. We were discussing which of them was better than the others and in what way.

"How many of them were there? One better, braver than another," Omar mused. "Maskhadov, Basayev, Geliskhanov, Raduyev, Israpilov, Umarov, Barayev . . . But for me, the best of all was Gelayev. Maskhadov had experience as a professional artilleryman, Basayev and Raduyev were unrivaled in daring, but the only one I trusted was Gelayev—I couldn't have entrusted my life to anyone else. I didn't want to be in anyone else's service. You go under someone's command, you kill and you're prepared to be killed, you empty your mind, you know nothing. And then you find out it was all in vain, you've just been risking your neck in a game, for someone else's advantage. There's treachery and deceit at every turn . . . so many good men were killed . . . all for nothing."

He had entirely lost faith and hadn't enlisted in another unit or gone off to another war. Living among people had become unbearable, so hard for him that, finally, he went off into the mountains and had lived at the herders' camp in the clearing ever since.

"What was Hamzat like?" I asked. Omar and everyone else in the gorge called Gelayev by the name he had adopted on his pilgrimage to Mecca.

"Sometimes you meet a man in whose hands you're willing to place your life because you know he'll make better use of it," he replied. "You want him to be the person who tells you what to do and how to live. Hamzat was just that sort of man."

Gelayev was famous, not just in Chechnya and the Pankisi Gorge, but all over the Caucasus, from Derbent to Sochi, like the imams who'd led uprisings in the past. It was said of him that whenever there was a major battle or an audacious armed raid in the Caucasus, the name Gelayev always featured among the heroes. No one knew what he'd done or who he'd thought of becoming before the war took possession of him. He was on the point of adult life when the great Soviet empire began to fall apart and the Caucasian provinces released from its control began to declare independence and mark out new borders.

Like many others, young and hotheaded, clueless about the world, he had let himself be carried away by the frenzy. He had answered the call of the Chechen president by reporting for service and enlisting in his army. He would soon prove better suited to it than almost anyone. His talent for soldiering immediately stood out, and he soon caught the eye of the president, who was making plans to send his best soldiers to neighboring wars to learn how to fight before they had to wage war in their own country. Gelayev went to support the Abkhazians, who had declared war on the Georgians in an effort to create their own, separate state. The help provided by the Chechen volunteers had been very useful. It was mainly thanks to them, and also the Russians, that the Abkhazians had succeeded in defeating the Georgians. By way of thanks, in keeping with military custom, they had allowed the Chechens to spend three days looting the city of Sukhumi, which they had captured. Years later, when fighting against the Russians, Gelayev had to take advantage of Georgian hospitality in the Pankisi Gorge, and he deeply regretted the fact that he'd let himself get roped into the Abkhazian affair, which had turned out to be a stratagem devised by Russian intelligence, aimed at oppressing the upstart Georgians and setting the Caucasian highlanders against one another.

But he had gained battle experience, and on returning to Chechnya, he became one of the president's top, most trusted commanders. Leading his own unit composed of veterans of the Abkhazian war, he suppressed rebellions incited by the president's enemies, and when Russia invaded Chechnya, he fought so bravely in all the major battles that he was said to be worth more in combat than half the insurgent commanders put together. Grozny, Argun, Samashki, Bamut, Gudermes, Shatoy—wherever he and his unit appeared, the Russian troops suffered their heaviest losses. In the mountains, he and the Saudi Arabian commander Khattab set an ambush for a powerful Russian tank column. They crushed it in less than a quarter of an hour, killing more than a hundred soldiers. But he had gained his greatest fame from his daring raid on Grozny when it was occupied by the Russians. The insurgents had recaptured the city, forcing the Russians to suspend the war and hold talks. Gelayev was the first of the insurgent emirs to be awarded Chechnya's top medal, "Pride of the Nation."

"To serve in Hamzat's unit was the greatest distinction. We were the elite; songs were sung about us." When Omar recalled those days, an indulgent smile appeared on his face, as if he couldn't believe that part of his life had really happened and that he still had a right to it. "In Hamzat's unit no one looted, and no one ever raised a hand to civilians. We didn't even take hostages for ransom."

During the two-year cease-fire, when the victorious emirs flew at one another's throats to seize the most power, the best positions and privileges, for themselves, Gelayev was the only one of the war heroes who did not tarnish his reputation. He stayed out of the political quarreling and intrigue, didn't get involved in dubious deals, and kept well away from the fratricidal fights that were constantly erupting. He did his best to avoid conflict, choosing instead to be on friendly terms with everyone. As soon as the war was over, he swore never to pick up a gun again, unless he had to defend his country against another Russian invasion. He remained true to his promise, even when Chechnya was on the brink of civil war. He refused to accept the post of minister of defense, claiming that if he took it on, sooner or later he'd have to turn against his own comrades and brothers. He rejected power and honors, underwent a religious conversion, and made a pilgrimage to Mecca. Disappointed by the freedom they'd won, which had increasingly metamorphosed into lawlessness and self-promotion by the emirs, the Chechens were casting longing looks in Gela-yev's direction and citing his name. They saw in him an austere but modest and upright man, a simple mujahid who shunned titles, wealth, and fame. The last honest man, their last hope of salvation.

"People saw him as an *abrek*," Omar said, and the young herders around the bonfire pricked up their ears. "If any of our emirs was like an *abrek*, it was Hamzat."

At one time in the Caucasus, the term *abrek* had been used to describe outcasts, wrongdoers, people who were hated, cursed, and dangerous. These men were driven out of the villages and valleys as a danger to others; they weren't capable of living in peace or of falling in line with everyone else, but refused to observe the rules that allowed the community to survive. Relatives, friends, and neighbors renounced them and shunned them like lepers.

That was tantamount to a death sentence, because for these cursed exiles, deprived of the support of the community, all that lay ahead in the merciless mountains was a lonely death as the result of hunger, cold, sickness, or suffering. Very few of them had the strength or courage to survive alone, far away from people, looking out for death with their heads held high, leading the life of outlaws and bandits—the *abreks*. But apart from prompting fear and condemnation, they also stirred plenty of envy or admiration, because they were brave enough to taste forbidden fruits and live as they wished.

"Those who chose to live by robbing and harming others were feared and hated. But people did sympathize with the unlucky ones whom a tangle of dreadful circumstances had condemned to the life of an outlaw. It was usually because they had caused bloodshed, and their crime had to be avenged, so they had become fugitives. But sometimes the reason for absconding was love, when their families wouldn't allow the lovers to be together." Sometimes Omar fell silent and stared into the crackling bonfire. At first, I thought he was looking for the right words, but when he automatically returned to his interrupted theme, I realized he'd been spinning this yarn for ages, repeating his story so often that he didn't need to scour his memory. "Nothing but wandering in the mountains, in the wilds, as solitary as a hermit, with no friends, no relatives, all of whom had abandoned them. No help or sympathy from any-where. And so on, to the day they died. They felt no fear of death because it was all they had to look forward to, the only thing that could free them from suffering. People described them as dead men in their lifetime, because although their hour had not yet struck, they were already lost to the living. The unlucky ones were pitied, but they had to pay the price for their crimes, or else people in the *auls* couldn't live in peace. But when the Russian Army appeared in the mountains bringing war with it, things changed."

The appearance of the Russians—the tsar's soldiers, imperial governors, officials, and Cossacks, Slavonic settlers who estab-lished farms and *stanitsas* (Cossack villages) in the Caucasian foreland—meant that instead of being outcasts and reprobates, the *abreks* became noble avengers, revered by the highlanders as heroes and defenders of the downtrodden. Like Joaquin Murrieta, the Californian outlaw who was supposedly the inspiration for Zorro, or Juraj Jánošík, the Slovak highwayman, both of whom were compared with Robin Hood of Sherwood Forest.

The new, foreign power oppressed and plundered the Caucasian highlanders, while the *abreks* organized ambushes and armed raids against the Cossacks, the military posts and patrols, the factories and banks, and the post coaches traveling through the mountain passes to Georgia. Increasingly, it wasn't highlanders who'd broken the village rules and customs who fled into the mountains to lead the lives of *abreks*, but people who'd rebelled against the Russians. And when armed insurgencies began to erupt in the Caucasus against the Russian authorities, many of the rebel leaders were seen as *abreks* too. In time, almost anyone who acted against Russia was called an *abrek*, and in the villages boys were named for them, so they'd grow up to be fearless warriors and heroes too.

"But traditionally the *abreks* didn't lead insurgencies—they never fought with others, always on their own," Omar said. "They'd take up arms when others began to have doubts and were ready to surrender. That was when the *abreks* appeared and took on an unequal fight, even when they knew they couldn't win and their cause was already lost."

When the Russians invaded Chechnya for the second time, although he realized that the feuding emirs wouldn't be capable of putting up resistance and couldn't win, Gelayev reached for the gun he'd put away long ago, formed a new unit, and went off to war. He turned out to have the largest army, of almost two thousand men. None of the other emirs had as many volunteers reporting to them for service. The commanders assigned him the task of defending the capital. But remembering their quarreling and discord, Gelayev no longer trusted them.

"He knew what he was doing. They wanted him to take the entire force of the Russian storm upon himself, while they bolted into the mountains to hide. Hamzat would have lost his men, and wouldn't have been able to stop the Russians anyway. So he only left a small unit to defend the city, while he and his army went up into the mountains to fight there." Omar was assigned to the defense of Grozny and was wounded during the fighting at Minutka. "The other emirs never forgave Gelayev for that. They were counting on throwing him to the Russkis to be killed, while they saved their own skins. And then they found they'd have to do the fighting and hiding from bombs. But they got their revenge, because when Hamzat and his unit reached the foreland from where they were going to drive into the mountains, the Russians were already waiting for them."

He had only managed to take refuge at his home village of Saadi-Kotar. For several weeks he had repelled the Russian attacks while trying to break through the siege at night. By the time he succeeded, he had lost half his army and the village had been reduced to rubble. With the survivors of his once-powerful force, he escaped into the mountains, but he couldn't find the safe hideouts that the other commanders were meant to have prepared for him for the winter. He was in no state to go on fighting, and the insurgent leaders branded him a traitor, demoted him from emir to private soldier, and stripped him of all his medals. Without much thought, he crossed into the Pankisi Gorge, where he gathered new troops, but went on fighting on his own, without relying on others.

He was tracked down in the mountains with a small unit of thirty or forty men. The Russians set a trap, flying in by helicopter. The insurgents scattered, but had no chance of escaping in the snow. Almost the entire unit was wiped out, and the few survivors were taken captive. Gelayev was killed by a shot from a machine gun mounted on the aircraft fuselage. The bullet ripped off his arm, and he died of blood loss. The insurgents who were taken prisoner identified his body, but the Russians refused to return it to his family, burying it in an unmarked grave, as they did with every Chechen emir's body.

"He died a martyr's death in solitude, just as an *abrek* should die. He had no friends because he had no equals. And friendship can only arise among equals. A real hero is always alone, and his life is marked by tragedy," Omar said, and everyone around the campfire knew that his story was at an end. "It might sound as if they were doomed to defeat, for who could have beaten an enemy one hundred times stronger? But the real victor is not the one who wins the battle, but the one who dies a proud and beautiful death in it. Eternal praise and peace be with them and their own place on earth."

He stopped talking, and silence fell around the campfire.

Six years earlier, here at the herdsmen's camp, Lara's sons, Shamil and Rashid, had heard Omar tell the same story.

Soon they went back to Europe, and the next year, only Rashid came to visit Lara. When she found out that this time her older son wasn't coming, Lara thought perhaps it was her fault, because of what she'd said during his last visit. She had told him off for turning up his nose at everything. She had refused to listen to his sermons about war, the just cause, the mujahideen and salvation, but perhaps she should have shown greater patience and allowed him to speak his heart. After all, it was just words, but to him, they were clearly important. Maybe she had hurt his feelings, maybe he felt rejected. She was terrified that she had lost him and that he'd never come back to see her again.

She thought through the conversations they'd had on the phone and over the computer, trying to remember the words he'd used, the tone of his voice, and his facial expression. Once upon a time, she'd been sure that although he could be secretive, she could see through him and knew him as well as she knew herself. But since leaving, he had become a mystery to her.

And so Rashid had come on his own. On the very first day, Lara asked him if he too could see how very much Shamil had changed; what was he missing so badly in Europe to want to keep on ranting about religion and war? Rashid shrugged and said he couldn't see anything wrong with his brother's behavior. So what if he wasn't always happy with his life? Who is? The main thing was that he found consolation at the mosque. And among the friends he'd met on the internet. She asked how that was done. He replied that you can meet and get to know people there who think the same way you do, who have the same likes and dislikes. You can chat, get things off your chest, and get advice. As in real life, but without leaving the house. That's how you meet people nowadays. It's better than having no kindred spirits and feeling all alone in the world.

"But he's got us," she said, still worried and wary. "I am far away, but he has you right there. What counts more than your family?"

"But it's because of his family that he hasn't come," Rashid replied, laughing.

She knew that Shamil's second child had been born, a son whom he'd named Rashid, for his brother. The baby was born prematurely and was weak and sickly. Apparently Shamil had decided to stay behind to help his wife. That was why he had canceled his trip to the Caucasus.

Rashid spent two weeks in the gorge, and his visit was quieter and more normal than the first one, a year ago, when both boys had come. And when she said good-bye to him at the airport, she no longer felt the despair that comes with parting. She felt cheerful and lighthearted—the time spent with her son had dispelled her fears. She saw him off as if he were getting on the bus to Akhmeta or Telavi, not flying to the other end of the world for God knows how long. She knew he'd be back—they'd both be back. Or at least she knew it was possible.

She stopped looking forward to the next vacation, and no longer crossed off the days in her calendar. She didn't worry when they said they weren't coming. They always had unexpected things to do, as happens in life. Rashid got married and had a son, then a second one. Soon after, Shamil's third son was born, then Rashid told her over the phone that his wife was expecting another child too, and that it would be another boy.

"You have to copy your brother in every way!" she joked. "Nothing but grandsons—I wish there were at least one little girl! Is there going to be a war or what?"

"We haven't finished yet," Rashid said, laughing.

He said that he and his wife hadn't yet decided what to name their son, but Shamil had chosen to give his own name to his youngest child.

"That's a good idea," Lara said. "Now, even when you two get old, I'll always have a little Shamil and a little Rashid."

She realized they weren't going to visit her in the gorge now. Obviously not—a bigger family meant greater expense, and neither of them was rolling in money. They often said that life in Europe wasn't cheap. She asked them not to send her money anymore, saying that she could cope—the local people wouldn't let her starve. She promised she'd come to see them in Europe, to help them out and finally get to enjoy her grandsons. She'd go, she definitely would. As soon as they'd picked the apples and grapes, as soon as they'd fetched in the firewood for the winter, as soon as their grandfather was better—lately he'd had pneumonia—or as soon as she'd saved up the cash.

They saw each other on the computer screen, and if the connection failed in Pankisi Gorge or there was a power outage, they talked on the phone. They knew there was no alternative, this would have to do. Well, such is life, that's how it goes. The main thing was that they hadn't lost their way in life. She'd forgotten all her fears and the bad thoughts that had kept her awake at night and ruined her sleep. She'd even stopped noticing Shamil's bitterness, though he still complained about his life, saying it was pointless and would come to nothing. She didn't respond, because he lost his temper if she tried to console him or tell him how much he had achieved and that many people would envy him the life he found so inadequate. She told herself he had his family to care for, and a household to maintain, so he had quite enough to worry about. They're right when they say nothing piles on the cares as much as your own children. And no one finds it easy to stop being young and enter adulthood.

She didn't even notice as four more years flew by from the time Shamil and Rashid came to visit. She didn't feel the burden of separation at all. She took care of the house and went to the cultural center in Duisi to sing old Kist songs with the other women. One day some foreigners came to the village. They knew who they were looking for because they had gone straight to the cultural center to ask about her. They said they were working for a world-famous French film director, a top award winner, who had decided to make a movie about the Chechen War. As there was still unrest on the northern side of the mountains, and in Georgia, visitors from Europe were given a friendly welcome, the director had decided that Chechnya would be represented in the movie by the Pankisi Gorge. They'd already made arrangements with the relevant authorities, and now they were looking for extras and actors for the supporting roles. They'd been told that Lara had trained as an actor and also performed onstage, so they'd come to ask if she could be persuaded to take part in the movie. Nothing hard to do—she'd be playing a Chechen woman who has fled the war. She'd be paid a suitable fee for the role. The movie was going to be titled *Separated*.

She said she'd have to think about it, but she knew at once that she'd agree. She immediately liked the title of the movie. So the dream she had long since given up for good was actually going to come true. That same day she decided to tell her sons about it. But she couldn't get through to either of them. It made her realize what a long time had passed since they'd last spoken to one another. Rashid was still in touch as before, but Shamil showed up on her computer screen at night less and less often. Sometimes she fell asleep waiting for him, and then his call woke her, and as soon as she answered he'd call softly from the screen: "Your guests are here!" He'd turn up like that, then disappear again for days, sometimes whole weeks on end.

Rather disappointed with her sons for spoiling her joy by not giving her the chance to share the news and her excitement, the next day she called again. But once again, nobody answered. She finally got an answer from Shamil's number on the third day, but it was his wife who picked up the phone. She said he wasn't there, he'd gone on a business trip to Belgium, he'd be back in a couple of days. But two days later when Lara called again, Shamil still wasn't at home.

"He came back and went off again, this time to Denmark," his wife said.

A few days after that, Lara was stopped at the market in Duisi by an old friend from school.

"My cousin's just back from Syria," she said. "He says he saw your Shamil there."

Lara was dumbstruck. She felt the blood drain from her face.

"In Syria? Impossible. He must have mistaken him for someone else," she managed to splutter. "Shamil's in Denmark, I spoke to him yesterday."

Now in its third year, the war in Syria was the world's worst ongoing conflict. Lara saw news of it every day on television. It had started innocently, like most wars, like the one in Grozny. Emboldened by the revolutions in Tunisia, Egypt, Yemen, and

Libya, where the tyrants had been deposed, the people had protested in the streets of Damascus as well. They too were shouting,
"Out! Out! Out!" "Never again!" and "Long live . . . !" But the
Syrian leader wasn't daunted by the crowd. Or maybe he wasn't
afraid to spill blood, though he did fear the loss of power, the
people's hatred, and his own death. He ordered the army to
shoot without mercy at anyone who marched in the streets to
demand his resignation. When the guns didn't help, he sent
tanks and bombers against the defenseless crowd. Finally, the
people had seized weapons too, and had formed an insurgent
army. The TV reports had said that in Damascus, Homs, and
Aleppo, thousands had been killed, tens of thousands, a hundred thousand, a quarter of a million people; millions had lost
their homes, and entire districts lay in ruins. The television
news presenter had said that in spite of the Syrians' misfortunes
and their appeals for aid, the world was helpless to stop the war
and put an end to the carnage. He also said that in response to
the world's indifference to the slaughter of Muslims, volunteers
were arriving in Syria from other Middle Eastern countries to
join the insurgents and fight against the tyrant from Damascus.

The people in the Kist villages had known about the Syrian
War for at least a year, ever since Gelayev's oldest son, Rustam,
was killed in it, the boy whose father had sent him to Cairo to
study. Gelayev was dead by the time the war in Syria began.
There was no one to stop Rustam; apparently his only dream
had been to be his father's equal, and he'd been waiting for
the chance. From Egypt, he had traveled to Syria, where he
had formed his own insurgent unit composed of other young
Chechens who were studying or working in the Middle East.

He and his entire unit were killed after just a few weeks, at a mosque in Aleppo that was bombarded during a night raid by government artillery.

Lara's sons, especially Shamil, had been friendly with Rustam at school, and after leaving the gorge, they had kept in touch, writing to each other and talking via their computers. She thought Shamil would be very upset about the news of his friend's death. "Two years younger than Shamil and one year older than Rashid," she calculated.

The story in the gorge was that lots of insurgents from the Caucasus had gone to the war in Syria. They'd left because they couldn't go on fighting against the Russians, who were so much stronger than they were and were always hunting them down, and also because the Syrian War had been declared a jihad. Taking part in it was the duty of every Muslim and would guarantee him salvation.

Some Kists from the Pankisi Gorge had gone to fight in Syria too. When Lara started questioning people, it turned out that at least a few young men from every single village had gone to Syria. Some of them used to attend the mosque in Duisi, and on setting out to join the war, they had said they were going to help their Muslim brothers fight their enemies and oppressors, the infidel, as they regarded the rulers of Syria. But very few of them had told their parents about their plans. Most had just disappeared without saying a word, or else they had put it around that they were going to Turkey to find work, as many young people from the gorge had done. But once across the Turkish border, they had turned off the road to Trabzon or Istanbul and headed south, into Syria. Some went there to fight in the holy cause, others to escape boredom and despair at home, and yet others in the hope of army wages and the spoils of war.

Without finishing her shopping, Lara went straight home from the bazaar. She didn't wait until evening, the usual time for her conversations with her sons, but called Shamil immediately. Once again, her daughter-in-law answered. This time, Lara wasn't surprised.

"But I had such a terrible weight on my heart, and my throat was so tight that I could hardly say a word. Sometimes you're desperate not to know everything."

Whenever she talked to me about her sons, she used the same words and phrases, the same definitions and similes, in the same order and with the same tone. I thought that perhaps her tendency to repeat it all from start to finish, the same facts in the same sequence, was part of her effort to understand what had really happened.

Her daughter-in-law told her she had missed Shamil again because he had just left the house and wouldn't be back until very late, too late to call.

"Don't lie to me," Lara said. "I know what's happened anyway."

Kheda burst into tears. It was the fourth time Shamil had gone to Syria, but he had forbidden her to mention it. "My mother mustn't know a thing! Swear on our children's heads that you won't tell her," he had insisted as he left, and then reminded her of her pledge every time he called.

"Tell him how I found out," Lara said, to reassure the girl. "Tell him someone saw him, and their relatives told me."

She also asked Kheda to tell Shamil that she was begging him to call her, and if it was possible in Syria, could they please meet as before on a computer screen. He couldn't refuse her that.

For three days she waited, hardly closing an eye, and keeping a lamp on at night so she could run to the computer as fast as possible without tripping over the furniture. On day four, Shamil appeared, half an hour after midnight. "Momma! Your guests are here!" she heard him say out of the darkness as soon as she answered his call. She leaped up and ran to the table. But the man talking in such a familiar voice and smiling at her indulgently from the computer screen was hardly recognizable as her son.

Now he had a long, straggly beard, shoulder-length hair, and a black scarf round his forehead with something written on it in Arabic. The way he was looking at her from the screen had changed too. At first Lara couldn't understand what exactly was different about it, until she suddenly thought of the faces of the insurgents she used to see in the gorge and of those men who had accosted her in Grozny outside the president's palace. There was a sort of arrogance in Shamil's eyes, a look of stubborn superiority. She stared at him in silence, lost for words, like the time they first saw each other after five years apart.

"Why on earth have you gone there, son?" she said, bursting into tears. "What the hell do you think you're doing?"

"Don't worry about me, I'm fine here," he said calmly. "It was necessary."

"Necessary? For whom? For you?"

"I had to do it. I'm a mujahid now, I have joined the path

that leads straight to the Almighty. It's a holy path. There's nothing more important in all the world."

"Didn't you think of me, your mother?"

"You should be pleased. I feel so happy here. For the first time in my life."

Then she said she wanted to come see him. In Syria. She wanted the joy of seeing him, she wanted to put her arms around him.

"You want to come here? But there's a war going on!"

"If you're all right there, I'll be all right too."

She was afraid he'd refuse to let her visit him or say it was impossible. He clearly didn't want her to come—she noticed the scowl of irritation that flashed across his face. When he was younger, he always made that face if she showed him affection in the presence of his friends. Irritated and embarrassed, he would tear free if she tried to hold his hand, or stiffen as she drew him toward her to kiss the top of his head. If only he'd agree! If only she could go see him. Then he would stop defying her. However grouchy he may have been, he was always obedient. He may not agree with his elders, but he always did as they said. And even if she couldn't convince him right away, she'd make enough fuss to get him out of there. After all, she was his mother. She'd bring him home and never let him go again. And next time, she'd keep a better eye on him. Anything to go fetch him! If only he'd agree!

"But it's madness!" he said, shaking his head in disbelief.

"Maybe it is, but you must at least do this one thing for me."

He said he would think about it, talk to the relevant people, and call her back tomorrow. He didn't call until the third day;

meanwhile she hadn't slept a wink, of course. He said all right, if she wanted to come see him she could, it could be arranged. In a couple of days he'd call again and tell her what to do.

"But when? When will you call? And when am I to come?" she asked frantically. She was afraid that the moment they stopped talking, he might change his mind about everything he'd agreed to. "Is there anything I can bring you? Tell me what you want."

She could tell he was softening—he was probably even smiling. Until now, his voice had seemed full of tension, dry and metallic, but suddenly it sounded warm, almost affectionate. He said he missed the taste of her *khinkali* dumplings, the way she made them at home. He'd never had any as good as hers.

"When I come, I'll make them for your lunch every day," she promised.

"Not for lunch—Ramadan is about to start, there'll be fasting during the day."

"Then I'll make extra *khinkali* for supper."

"For supper, that would be good."

He also asked for preserved fruit and pickles. And cottage cheese, the kind the shepherds made at Omar's camp in the mountains.

"And please bring some *churchkhela*. For the commander," he added. "It slipped my mind, but he asked for it specially."

At once, she could see the two of them, Shamil and Rashid, brawny adult men, sitting at the kitchen table eating *churchkhela*, nuts strung on a thread and dipped in a fast-setting blend of grape juice, corn flour, and sugar. The Kists kept *churchkhela* at home as candy, but they also took it on long journeys and trips into the mountains as high-energy food.

She was so excited by what Shamil had said, and so delighted by his unexpected homesickness, that she didn't stop to wonder about his request for a gift for the commander. It never occurred to her that if the commander was asking for a Kakhetian treat, he might be from their part of the world too.

"I'll bring it, you bet I will!" was all she said.

She clung firmly to the idea that all she had to do was take her son everything he missed and liked, and tempted by her gifts, he'd drop his new, incomprehensible life and return to his old one. Then everything would be as before. Everything would be all right.

"From Tbilisi, get on the bus to Istanbul, but first make sure it's the one that stops at Aksaray station. Don't get off until there. It's the last stop. Don't forget—Aksaray." He repeated it over and over. Lara was so overcome with joy that he was worried about her. She hadn't stopped to think at all, nor had she asked him any questions about the dangers she might meet along the way. She was thrilled by the idea that Shamil was concerned about her, because that meant he wasn't indifferent to everything, and perhaps he wasn't ready to take his leave of this world yet.

Her cousin Ali drove her to the station. He borrowed a car so she wouldn't have to lug her heavy bags. She wasn't taking much for herself, but she had stuffed a suitcase and a large bag made of strong canvas with gifts and groceries for her son. Before leaving, she checked the weight of her luggage—sixty-six pounds.

"Why on earth are you taking so much stuff?" Ali said, grimacing as he hauled her suitcase down the stairs. "You'll pull your arms off."

"I'll manage," she mumbled. "I'm sure there'll be kind people to help me."

The days since her final conversation with Shamil had gone by in a flash. She couldn't remember what she'd done, whom she'd seen, or what had happened. All she could think about was the journey. She couldn't wait to meet up with her son, but she was also scared of what lay ahead of her. She couldn't focus on anything. She was worried about whether she'd cope along the way. She'd never gone so far from home before—in fact, she'd never been anywhere except Tbilisi and Grozny.

When the day of her departure finally came, and Ali drove up to the house, she checked a hundred times to make sure all the documents she needed for the journey were in her purse and, once again, counted the $420 she'd borrowed from various neighbors. She glanced into her wallet to be certain the piece of paper with the long phone numbers Shamil had dictated to her was still in there, folded in four. She had tried to memorize them, but she couldn't concentrate, so she couldn't get the series of figures to stick in her mind. She ran her gaze down the rows of letters and numbers again. "Phone numbers in Istanbul," "phone numbers in Gaziantep," "phone numbers in Syria."

"Don't be afraid, and don't worry about a thing. If anything goes wrong, you can call," he'd done his best to reassure her.

These phone numbers, like secret passwords, were meant to guide her to Shamil, so she had to guard them like the greatest treasure.

"There'll be someone waiting for you at every point," he said.

"Not you?" she asked.

"In Istanbul?" he said, laughing nervously, as if about to lose patience. "We'll meet here, at my place in Syria."

It occurred to Lara that, not so long ago, that was how he'd referred to his home in the Alps. It felt like only yesterday when he'd said, "At our place in Europe."

The ticket cost almost fifty dollars, and the bus was to leave before noon. At the ticket desk she asked how long the journey would last and was told it could take one and a half days. She said good-bye to Ali and took her seat by the window. She saw him checking to make sure the driver had stowed her case and bag in the luggage compartment. He waved to her again, turned away, and vanished into the crowd. Now she was on her own.

The bus was filling up with passengers. A young foreigner came and sat next to Lara. She had messy fair hair, cut short like a boy's. Her denim pants, with pockets sewn onto the legs, and her heavy boots designed for hiking in the mountains made her look like a boy too. She had small breasts hidden beneath her loose shirt and slender, narrow hips. Despite the hot weather, she had a freshness about her, and Lara guessed that the girl's slight body must be concealing a great love of life, because that's what gives a person such a glow. She tried to remember when she had lost her own glow, but she couldn't work it out. Perhaps she hadn't lost it for any particular reason, but had just mislaid it somewhere along the way. She was just a mother. She hadn't nurtured her own love of life, she'd never thought it could vanish irretrievably, and she'd have to carry on without it. The girl smiled radiantly, infectiously, and that made Lara feel sure she still loved life, too.

"Georgian?" the girl asked.

Lara said yes.

"Georgian, that's great. Really great," the girl stammered in Russian. She couldn't speak it properly, or Georgian, let alone Chechen.

And Lara knew none of the languages of Europe, which must have been where the girl was from.

"Turkey? Business? Friends?" she asked.

"Friends," Lara replied.

"I, home . . ." the girl said, smiling happily. "Five months," she added, splaying her fingers for Lara to see.

So she hadn't been home in all that time.

Lara had seen young women like her, from Europe and America, touring the world, because they came to Georgia too, and even visited the gorge. It was with them in mind that she was planning to open a guesthouse. They went hiking in the mountains, spent weeks at a time living in shepherds' huts, caught trout in the mountain streams, and went on bear hunts. Lara had heard that some of these visitors had been asking if anyone in the local villages was interested in selling their house.

Sometimes she wondered what these young people were looking for on their travels. What was missing for them at home? They had so much of everything there, didn't they? That's what Shamil had said: Every wish could come true. You just had to have one. Yet something drove them out into the world. Was it a longing or a fear? The Kists found it hard to believe the visitors from Europe could want to settle in a place the locals were desperate to escape as fast as possible because they saw no hope of a good and worthwhile life there. Whereas those people had left their life in Europe for the same reason, insisting it was nothing but an endless race to increase your property or a comfortable but ultimately meaningless waste of time. What some saw as the Promised Land was for others a land of disappointment and lost dreams, a waste of time. Who'd have guessed?

She glanced over her shoulder at the girl, who had fallen asleep with her head dropped to her chest. Lara was tempted to position her more comfortably against the armrest. As soon as the bus had left, the girl had taken off her boots and tucked her small feet on the seat under her. Like a child. What would Shamil have thought of her? Alone, without a man, dressed like a boy and behaving like a boy. When the bus stopped for a short break, Lara saw her smoking a cigarette. Shamil probably wouldn't have liked that. He didn't smoke tobacco or drink wine—he said it was a sin. But that was in the gorge, among Muslims. Did it bother him in Europe too?

They passed Batumi and made a long stop on the Turkish border. Ali, who had been to Turkey in search of casual labor, had warned her that the customs clearance and luggage inspection could take a few hours and that it was better to drive to the border, cross it on foot alone, and then get on a bus or find a taxi on the other side. She said she'd prefer to carry on without changing vehicles. How could she trudge around with all that luggage? The moment you get out, you're lost. Shamil had told her to go all the way to Aksaray station, in Istanbul, without getting off the bus anywhere before that, so that's what she was going to do. So what if she had to wait longer at the border? She was going to fetch her son, to rescue him from the war. That was all that mattered.

Beyond the Turkish border, at first she looked at the great big world with curiosity—she'd never seen it before. She stared at the villages and towns they passed, the people and the land-scape. But somehow life in the outside world didn't seem terribly different from life in Pankisi Gorge. That was a little disappointing but also reassuring.

Gradually, tired by the heat and the rigors of the journey, Lara sank into a torpid state; the scenery slowly faded, and she lost track of time. Now it was as if they'd only just set off, but moments later, she felt she'd been traveling for all eternity. Now she was filled with joy that soon she'd be seeing her son, but in minutes she began to panic that she wasn't going to get there, she'd never find him and would fail to achieve any of her plans. She fell asleep in broad daylight, but by the time she woke, it was night. At dawn she dozed off again, but the next time she opened her eyes, she noticed that the passengers were wide awake, busy straightening their clothes and seeing to their luggage. Finally, they drove into a huge city, the biggest she had ever seen. The bus slowed down, and as she gazed out the window, Lara felt as if they were gliding down the middle of a rushing river of cars and people, amid a tumult of horns, engines roaring, and people shouting. They drove onto a large bridge across a stretch of water so wide she couldn't see its banks.

"The Bosporus," the girl sitting next to her said, pointing out the window. "Europe."

"Europe," Lara said to herself automatically, "so this is Europe."

When the bus finally rolled into Aksaray station, she was the last passenger to get off. She dragged out her case and bag and stuffed them under a bench by the bus stop. She sat down and hesitantly looked around. They were meant to be waiting for her here—that's what Shamil had said. Someone was supposed to come up and ask if she was Abu Mohammed's mother. That's what he was named now, in Syria.

She'd been sitting there for quite a while, feeling increasingly worried, tired by her uncomfortable journey, her legs aching and swollen. The crowd of people buzzing around the station oppressed and overwhelmed her, as did the strange, unfamiliar noises. She was scared she wouldn't be recognized. She was wearing a hijab, as Shamil had told her to. She had put it on in the bus, just after crossing the Turkish border. The large scarf wrapped around her head left only her face exposed. How was her son's courier going to pick her out of the crowd in this outfit?

Whenever she heard one of the passers-by speaking in a Caucasian language, she tried talking to them. She figured a Circassian, Lezgin, Armenian, or Azerbaijani must also know Russian, so she could ask them a question, get some advice, and then she wouldn't be so alone. Finally, she plaintively began to ask everyone and anyone for help in Russian. But the people just shook their heads and hurried onward. She was feeling frantic when, at last, she noticed a bearded young man looking at her. After a brief hesitation, he came up and asked her a question in an unfamiliar language. He repeated it and then, without waiting for an answer, made signs to tell her to stay put. He took a phone from his pocket and made a call. He spoke a few sentences and then handed her the phone.

"*Shishani?* You Chechen woman?" she heard. It was a man's voice, talking in broken Russian, the way the Arabs she'd met in the gorge spoke it. And *shishani*—that was what they called the Chechens. "Are you the mother of Abu Mohammed?"

"Yes, he's my son," she replied, and felt the last of her strength draining away.

"Go with the man and do as he tells you. Don't worry. You'll be seeing Abu Mohammed soon."

The bearded man picked up her luggage and told her to follow him. They went outside, into the street, so busy and noisy that it made Lara's head spin. The man hailed a taxi. He'd brightened up now, like a student who has solved a difficult problem in front of the whole class and knows he's going to be praised for it. Throughout the ride, he talked to the taxi driver. He also turned to Lara, smiled, and said something to her in his own language, which she couldn't understand.

"*Shishani* okay," he said, nodding. "Abu Mohammed okay."

She returned his smile and no longer felt afraid.

They arrived at another bus station, where he paid the taxi driver and told her to follow him. At the ticket office, he bought her a ticket and took her to the right stop. He waited until the bus arrived to collect the passengers, loaded her luggage on board, escorted her to the entrance, and pointed at a sign on the front window. "Gaziantep," he read out aloud. He helped her to get on board and sat her in her place. Lara noticed that as he was leaving, he pressed a roll of banknotes into the driver's hand. He turned around, smiling, and waved goodbye to her.

She didn't know where the city of Gaziantep was or how long a journey she still had ahead of her. If she had known it would last all night and most of the next day, twenty hours altogether, she'd probably have burst into tears. She'd never been so tired, at the limit of her strength and endurance. Her clothes clung to her, sticky with sweat. She didn't speak a word for the entire duration of the journey, and she couldn't remember much about it, except the great effort she put into keeping her self-control and not bursting into tears in front of strangers.

Numb and semiconscious, when the bus finally reached its destination she struggled to get out of her seat. She staggered off the bus, clinging to the armrests, limping at each step like an invalid, crushed by illness and old age. *This has to be the end*, she kept telling herself. *Shamil will appear at any moment.* The driver dragged out her luggage. She hadn't the strength to haul her case and bag into the station waiting room, so she left them at the stop and sat heavily on a bench, surrendering to fate.

She didn't have to wait long. This time, Shamil's courier found her instantly. She saw the man approaching and knew it was him. She felt as if it had all happened before, and she was meeting him for the second time. The courier here at the bus station in Gaziantep looked exactly like the one in Istanbul— young, with long hair and a black beard. He too addressed her in a foreign language, then took out a phone and made a call. She held out a hand, knowing he was about to pass it to her. And again she heard a voice speaking with an Arabic accent, asking the same questions. *Shishani?* Are you the Chechen woman? Are you the mother of Abu Mohammed?

"Where is my son?" she asked with an effort.

"Tomorrow, it's late now, there's no connection."

"I've come to see my son."

"Tomorrow, tomorrow after dinner, everything's okay."

The young man took her luggage and gestured for her to follow him. Only now did she feel how hot it was here. She had never experienced such intense heat before. The air was so stuffy that she couldn't breathe. She barely managed to drag herself to the car waiting for them outside the bus station.

The drive across the busy city took another hour.

"*Saray*," said the young man, pointing at a large building as they stopped outside it.

The hall and the inner courtyard were swarming with people coming and going, jostling and bumping into each other, shouting and wailing—men, women, and children.

The man led her upstairs to a large room that looked like a school assembly hall. He indicated that she was to wait for him. The air was not as close in here, and the heat wasn't quite as oppressive either. Outside, her eyes had been dazzled by the sun, but once they had adjusted to the gloom in here, she saw tables with computers standing in a row against one of the walls. There were about a dozen Arabs in field uniforms hovering by them. They looked just like the volunteers from the Middle East who had pitched camp with the Chechen insurgents in the Pankisi Gorge. *Mujahideen*, Lara thought. As she sat and observed them, she noticed that some of them were staring at the shining screens and writing something, while others were moving between the first and second floors, guiding people up the stairs. They were mainly young men, though now and then women in hijabs appeared. The Arabs sat them on chairs in front of the computers, asked some questions, and wrote things down, like the clerks at the local administration. Lara was surprised to see that after each conversation, the mujahideen shook hands with the new arrival, as if congratulating them on something, and finished off by posing for a photograph with them. As they did so, they raised an index finger in the air as a sign that there is only one God in heaven.

Her guide returned and took her upstairs to the third floor, where in a long, dark passage he knocked at one of the doors. A woman in a headscarf opened it. The young man said something to her while glancing at Lara. The woman nodded and opened the door wide to invite her in. The young man put Lara's luggage in the room and was gone without another word.

The room was tiny, cluttered with mattresses, pots, plates, and bundles strewn around the floor.

"*Suriya,*" the woman said.

Intrigued, Lara took a closer look at her. Syria. She guessed the woman had escaped from the war. She had never met anyone from that country, for which her son was prepared to die. *Maybe she's seen him . . .*

Apart from the woman, there were three little girls in the room who looked like her daughters. The woman said something to them in Arabic, and they cleared one of the mattresses. Lara realized she was to spend the night here. Although dusk was falling, the heat hadn't eased, and Lara was still bothered by it. She took off her headscarf, but that brought no respite either. The room had small windows like arrow slits close to the ceiling. There was no way of reaching them. But Lara was sure she would faint if she didn't get some fresh air immediately.

She went into the passage and spotted a door onto the balcony surrounding the courtyard. She pressed the handle and opened it. A wave of hot air struck her in the face, but she felt relief and slowly regained her composure.

From the courtyard, she heard a shrill howl. She looked down and realized that there was a field hospital below. Lying on metal beds, under the open sky, were sick and wounded men in blood-stained bandages, with arms or legs missing, groaning in pain and crying for help. Some of the patients were wearing uniforms.

Suddenly she felt a tug at her sleeve. Clearly agitated, the woman hosting her for the night was pulling on her arm while pointing at Lara's hair and at the wounded men in the court-yard. Lara was terrified that she'd seen something she shouldn't have and that something bad had happened that would foil her efforts and prevent her from meeting with her son. The Arab woman went on shouting, tugging at Lara's hair, and then pushed her inside from the balcony.

"*Haram*," she cried, wagging a finger, once they were back in the room.

Lara remembered that before going out onto the balcony she had taken off her headscarf. She had shown herself to strange men with her hair uncovered, which Muslim women were not allowed to do.

The muezzin call to evening prayer reminded her that it was Ramadan, the holy month of fasting and atonement, designed to help the faithful distinguish truth from falsehood and deserve forgiveness of their sins and eternal salvation. Lara thought it a good sign—perhaps it was the best time for a journey like hers.

Darkness fell. Her Arab hostess lighted candles and set about preparing supper. Nightfall broke the fast. Listening to her bustling around quietly, Lara realized she'd had nothing to eat or drink since crossing the Turkish border. But she didn't feel hungry or thirsty. She just wanted the night to be over as fast as possible and for the next day to begin, the day she was going to see Shamil. She was exhausted and ached all over, especially in her swollen legs. Without undressing, she lay down on the mattress, though she knew she wouldn't sleep at all. *If I can just get through the night*, she kept telling herself as she lay there with her eyes open. *He's so close now.*

She felt someone tugging at her sleeve and opened her eyes. The smallest of the little girls was kneeling beside her, holding out a bent tin plate with a triangular piece of fresh baklava on it. Dripping with syrup, the pastry smelled of pistachios and honey.

"*Iftar*," the little girl said.

Next morning, when the guide came to fetch her, Lara was sitting on the mattress, long since dressed, packed, and ready to continue her journey. She had yearned so badly for that moment to arrive that she couldn't even feel the heat that set in as soon as the sun rose. Now she didn't feel tired or in need of sleep. She kept promising herself she'd be patient and strong, but the prolonged anticipation was beyond her strength. She was afraid she was wasting time, that every second of delay meant a danger that things could go wrong, and that something would hold her up again.

They went down a floor to the computer room, where she'd

waited the day before. From early morning it was full of people, and the Arab mujahideen were registering new arrivals. Once again, she couldn't help feeling she'd been through this whole experience before and that it would keep recurring into infinity, she'd never get out of this time loop, never see Shamil, fail to save him from death, and nobody would ever find her either, she'd be stuck here forever.

"*Shishani, shishani,*" she heard. She turned her head. An Arab in a ragged tunic pointed out some young men waiting in the passage for their turn to register at the computer terminals. Immersed in her own fears and vacillations, she hadn't noticed that the young men—there were five of them, and they looked like teenagers—were glancing at her as if they wanted to talk to her but weren't bold enough and were waiting for a prompt from her.

"Are you from our part of the world?" she asked in Chechen.

Eagerly, they said yes. They took it as an invitation and came up to her, looking at her with unconcealed curiosity.

"We're from Gudermes," explained the smallest, who looked older than the others. "Is it true you're the mother of Abu Mohammed?" he immediately asked.

"Do you know my son?" she replied, surprised by the question.

"Abu Mohammed? Who doesn't know him!" the Chechen said, amazed. They knew Shamil from the videos the mujahideen posted on their websites, in which the jihadists spoke about the war in Syria, encouraging volunteers to come enlist in their army. Other mujahideen shielded their faces while talking about the war, for fear of being recognized. Abu Mohammed was one of the few who spoke openly, without hiding from anyone.

"My Shamil?" She couldn't believe it.

"Abu Mohammed," the Chechen hesitantly corrected her. "We didn't trust the others, but we believed every word of Abu Mohammed."

They were curious to know if she really was on her way to Syria to visit her son, and when she confirmed it, they nodded with approval.

"But I'm not going for a visit, just to take him home, away from the war," she said.

They burst into laughter, as if she had said something funny. It made her lose her temper.

"What about you? What are you looking for out there?" she asked angrily. "Do your mothers and fathers know you're here?"

They laughed again. The smallest and oldest, who had already spoken to her, replied that he'd told his parents he was going to Turkey to look for work. They believed him. He was twenty, and without asking his opinion, they had arranged for him to marry a girl from the next village. It hadn't even occurred to his father that he might be acting against the boy's wishes. The boy had been talking to his friends for ages about enlisting for the war in Syria. Plenty of Chechen boys had gone already—they knew from them what to expect out there.

He said he didn't want to speak for the others, but he knew many of them had gone to Syria guided by their faith. Of course it was a good thing to serve a rightful cause, though, in his case, by his own honest admission, he had come to gain an important experience in life, but also in the hope of making money. He had heard that in the war in Syria, the jihadists were allowed to loot, and many of them were doing so. Then they were exporting the goods to Turkey, selling them, and going home to the Caucasus with hard cash, or sending the money home. It was easy to find buyers for their trophies—here in Gaziantep, for instance. They came forward and asked of their own accord, or even placed specific orders. And if you struck a good bargain, they might pay a deposit too. He'd also heard that in some insurgent units they paid a regular wage, like in the army, and were happy to accept Chechens because they regarded them as born warriors, one of whom was worth a hundred Arabs. He knew that many people would frown on him for going to war for money, but what was the difference between working as an insurgent and working as a regular soldier? If he were an army captain or a sergeant, nobody would point a finger at him for making a living out of soldiering. How was being with the insurgents any worse? As good a wage as any other. Better than slaving away on building sites or in the fields.

Another of the Chechens, a younger boy, had told his parents that he needed money to go study in Europe. They had borrowed dollars from within the family, and he'd used them to buy a ticket to Istanbul. He hadn't told them the truth because they would have tried to stop him—they'd have taken away his passport—but he believed that for a Muslim, participating in a war like the one in Syria was a sacred duty. That was what her son Abu Mohammed said on the recruiting videos. He wanted to fight on the side of his Muslim brothers and sisters against the godless Bashar Assad from Damascus and his army.

"Did any of you think of your mothers?" she said, hearing a latent, pleading note in her own voice, and that angered her. "They brought you into the world. You owe obedience to them, not the emirs. God will punish you for the wrongs you are doing them. Your sacrifice won't please Him at all."

She wanted to add that the Koran forbade treating your mother like that, but she stopped herself in time. They probably knew the Holy Scripture in detail, definitely better than she did. So all she said was that disobeying your mother was a cardinal sin, and then the conversation broke off, because the Arabs sitting at the computers summoned the Chechens over. The young men went and sat down at tables to fill in forms and then stood with the mujahideen for photographs as proof of a successful enlistment. Later on, she found out that for each photograph with a new conscript, the recruiters received a payment. One of the Arabs came up to Lara and, without saying a word, handed her a telephone.

"It's Shamil. They're going to bring you to me right away," she heard her son's voice through the receiver.

The Arab mujahideen collected Lara and the five Chechens and escorted them outside, where a minibus and its driver were waiting for them. They told them to take all their things with them. After a half-hour drive, they stopped, and the Arabs told them to transfer to two passenger cars. Another fifteen minutes, maybe more, and they stopped again. This time they were told to get out and take their luggage with them.

"This is the border," one of the Chechens said quietly.

They were led to a low barrack. Outside it, they were separated. The Chechens were told to get into another car, which immediately drove off. A dark-skinned man came up to Lara and instructed her to go inside the barrack and wait until he came for her. Once again, she was alone, and her fear and uncertainty returned. As they got out of the car, the Chechens had pointed at a chicken-wire fence visible in the distance. Only that far to go now, just those few hundred yards divided her from the place where Shamil was waiting for her.

The barrack was in semi-darkness, but she spotted a wooden bench against the wall and a woman sitting on it. She looked like a Chechen. She was wearing a flowery headscarf tied just as the Caucasian village women usually tied theirs.

"Going to your son?" the woman asked in Russian.

"Yes, my son." Lara sighed.

"They'll let you in?"

"I think so, he called to say he's waiting."

"Then you're lucky. Mine refuses to see me. I've been waiting here for nine days, but every day he calls to tell them not to let me through."

The dark-skinned Arab appeared in the doorway. He nodded to Lara and gestured as if to tell her to continue on her own, straight ahead.

"Go, go, before yours changes his mind too," the woman said.

Lugging her heavy bags, Lara trailed toward the Syrian border, ever nearer and more visible. Now she could see not just the chicken-wire fence but some people standing behind it too. And a heavy iron gate through which the road led into Syria. There was just one, final frontier post separating her from it, where uniformed men were checking travel documents. She handed over her passport, and the soldier slowly turned the pages. He looked up and asked her a question. She couldn't understand. He repeated it, impatiently this time.

"*Shishani, shishani*," she automatically mumbled.

He barked something else at her, waving her passport under her nose.

"No visa," he hissed and tossed the passport to the floor.

She picked it up and obligingly handed it to him again. Again he hurled the booklet to the floor and showed Lara that she had to leave, that he wasn't letting her through the gate into Syria.

She fell on her knees before him, begging, sobbing, and trying to grasp his hand. Her lament changed into howling, a wail of despair.

"Help me!" she pleaded. "Does anyone here speak Chechen? Or Russian? Somebody, please help me!"

There was confusion, and some soldiers came running. Soon, one of them approached her with a cell phone.

"What do you need, lady?" someone asked down the phone in Russian with an Arabic accent.

"My son! I'm going to my son, but they won't let me through. His name is Abu Mohammed! *Shishani!*" she cried into the receiver.

"Don't worry, everything's going to be fine."

He told her to hand the phone to the commander of the frontier post. They talked for a while, and then the officer waved her onward.

As she walked toward the iron gate, she felt she was crossing something much more important and more ominous than the line dividing the territories of two separate countries. She was entering a world she didn't want to know and that didn't interest her. If it were up to her, she'd rather not know it existed at all. She glanced fearfully at the people clinging to the wire fence on the other side. They looked as if they were in a cage, dangerous, uncivilized, like wild animals. She was horrified at the thought that once she stepped through the gate, she'd be among them.

She walked through and stopped on the Syrian side, trying to spot Shamil in the crowd. He was meant to be here waiting for her. Had something happened? Hadn't he come? She searched for him, scanning the men's faces. They all looked identical to her, gray with dust, ragged and unshaven. Could it be that she didn't recognize her own son? Her heart began to pound as if trying to leap out of her chest.

She didn't spot him. It was he who saw her, the moment she stopped in the open gate. He saw her looking around, trying to find him, bending under the weight of her luggage. She didn't even notice him when he was already walking toward her, pushing his way through the crowd. Only when he stood right next to her and laid a hand on her arm did she look at him in surprise and horror. She couldn't believe she hadn't noticed him approaching, or that she hadn't sensed his presence.

He hugged her tight, and she burst into tears.

"It's all right now." He stroked her cheek. "We're going home, you can rest."

She trudged after him, staring underfoot for fear of tripping and falling over. When she looked up, she saw Shamil's back ahead of her. He was wearing a soldier's vest over a long blue cotton shirt and baggy pants. She'd never seen him dressed like that before. Nor had she ever seen him with a weapon, but now he was carrying a machine gun slung over his shoulder like a sports bag.

People stepped aside to let him pass, as for an important person, to whom precedence and respect were due. When he stopped at an enormous car, six other insurgents jumped out to meet him, all young and bearded, with long hair and guns. At the sight of them, the crowd of onlookers that had gathered around the vehicle stepped back a few paces.

"And here are my brothers," Shamil said. "From Chechnya, nothing but our people, like at home."

He sat in front behind the wheel and placed her on the large backseat, which was upholstered in soft leather and as comfortable as the couch in a palace. The whole car, as big as a house, shone with wealth and splendor.

"Is this your car?" she asked.

"Mine?" Shamil said, amused. "The only thing here that's mine is the shirt on my back. I got the car from the emir. He lent it to me when he found out you were coming. It's armor-plated, by special request, they brought it for him all the way from Iran. He only lets me touch it. He doesn't trust anyone else, but he has faith in me not to put a bomb under the seat."

He said she'd meet the emir in person, because he'd promised to visit. But maybe she knew him already? Or had at least seen him? He was from the gorge—he grew up in the next village, Birkiani.

"He's from Birkiani?" she asked in amazement. "What's his name?"

"He calls himself Abu Omar," he said. "But here they call all of us *shishani*."

"Abu Omar?" she repeated.

"Everyone here knows him. He distinguished himself in the

war like few others. An important figure, and I'm on his staff, I'm his adjutant and interpreter. The emir can only speak Georgian and Russian—even his Chechen is poor. You'll see him tomorrow because he's coming by in the evening."

The radiophone began to crackle. Shamil picked up the receiver and said in Chechen, "We're off."

"That's to the men in the other car," he explained. "That's how we drive here, always in two cars, for safety. If something happens to one of them, the other can help."

They were driving fast, aggressively, as if racing against someone. The blazing heat, the stuffy air, and all the noises were now behind the tightly closed windows. They rushed headlong across the dirty, stony, gray desert. Then they turned onto a surfaced road and raced even faster, passing wagons harnessed to camels or donkeys and huge trucks loaded with pyramids of luggage.

The yellow sky was wreathed in heavy, pitch-black smoke. Lara tried to work out where it was coming from, but all she could see were piles of burning trash heaped along the road. She could see men standing by the roadside in flowing tunics. The scarves and turbans wound around their heads made them look like figures without faces.

"Is there something burning?" she asked Shamil.

"There's always something burning," he said. "Planes fly in at night and drop bombs."

Only when they drove in among the first buildings did she see the devastation caused by the war—blown-up houses reduced to rubble in narrow alleys where, before the war, traders had set up their stalls, roofs hanging off, walls cracked by shells, the empty holes of windows blackened by fire, crushed and burned-out cars. And people, evidently still living among the charred ruins and hovels that were the remains of their town. There was a whole swarm of them. Why hadn't they fled when the first bombs fell? What were they hoping for? Now they were drifting among the skeletons of their former homes, clearing the rubble from what had once been backstreets and gateways, digging in the ruins, and chasing away herds of stray goats and packs of feral dogs. In the cloud of gray-and-white dust that hung over the bomb site, they looked like the ghosts of the damned, condemned to eternal wandering, never to know peace again.

"It's dreadful here," she whispered, looking out the window.

"What do you mean? It's only here that I know why I'm alive," Shamil said from the front seat.

"It's like hell on earth," she added, as if she hadn't heard him.

"And from here, I intend to go straight to heaven."

He explained that the city they were driving into was called Aleppo, but they were stopping in the remote suburbs because Assad's troops were stationed ahead, and there was street fighting. He said it was one of the oldest and most famous cities in the entire Arab world. And that it had been home to the largest covered market in the world, but that had been destroyed, along with the rest of the old city, its caravansary, baths, and mosques, by the troops of the tyrant from Damascus, the infidel Assad, for whom nothing was sacred except power.

They drove for a good hour—through the canyons of ruined buildings and then through busy, prosperous districts untouched by the war. Finally they stopped outside a high stone wall surrounding a two-story house. Still in the car, Shamil announced his imminent arrival over the radiophone, and the minute they slowed down before the gate, a guard opened it wide and then closed it as soon as they'd driven inside.

The house was magnificent, like a sultan's palace. There was a large courtyard paved with stone mosaics, with date palms growing inside it and water babbling in a small pond. Shaded galleries gave a pleasant view onto it and led into rooms clad in white marble on the first and second floors.

Stunned by the elegance and splendor, Lara looked around her, not knowing where to rest her gaze first.

"It's like the garden of paradise, isn't it? There are lots of places like this in the neighborhood. Rich people used to live here," Shamil said. "This house belongs to a friend of mine, a mujahid. He devoted his life to the jihad and has been fighting for twenty years. Mainly in Afghanistan. He bought this place when he married a local woman. When I told him my mother was coming to see me, he told me to bring you here and took his wife and children to her family home in the countryside. We have the house to ourselves for a whole week, so you'll be able to rest."

"I'm barely alive," she said, sighing with relief. "It's my third day on the road . . ."

"So you probably won't manage to make *khinkali* for this evening . . ."

"Maybe tomorrow? I can't feel my legs . . ."

"Tough," he said. "It's a bit of a pity. I shouldn't have told my friends that because you were coming there'd be Georgian dumplings for supper. I even bought lamb specially . . ."

He was disappointed, and he couldn't hide it. *Like a child*, Lara thought.

"Are there a lot of them coming?" she asked.

"Sixteen. All from Chechnya. They'll be here after prayers, when it gets dark."

"I'll make you *khinkali*, I'll manage, I just have to knead the dough," she said. "I'll make everything you want."

At once he cheered up.

"The sisters should be here soon, they'll help you with the dough."

"Sisters?"

"The girls. They come here for the jihad too, not just men," he explained. "You'll see for yourself."

He led her upstairs to a room that was to be her bedroom. She unpacked her things, freshened up, rested a while, and when she went downstairs there were three girls bustling around the kitchen. They were startled at the sight of her, as if she'd caught them doing something they shouldn't. In identical black hijabs and grayish tunics, they looked like students in school uniforms. Two of them stuck together, like sisters. The third spoke to Lara in Chechen.

"So you are Abu Mohammed's mother?"

She said to call her Ayesha and not to be upset if she didn't reply at once, because it was a new name—she'd only adopted it here in Aleppo, and wasn't yet used to it. In Holland, in Europe, where she and her parents had moved from the Caucasus, her name had been Fatima.

"What sort of strange fashion is this? Do you all change your names to new ones here?" Lara said in amazement.

"Almost all of us. Some for safety, so no one will find out where they've been and what they were doing when they return home. And others, like me, to have a new name for their new life. Because we're starting a new life here, we're becoming different people."

"And what have you come here for? In search of a new life? In the middle of a war? A girl?"

"The jihad isn't just a war. You can serve it in various ways, in the kitchen, for instance."

"What about them?" Lara said, glancing at the two girls standing by the wall. "Are they ours too?"

"They're French," Ayesha said. "I mean they're Arabs, but from Paris."

They got down to work. Lara and Ayesha kneaded dough for *khinkali*, and once it was ready, they made pouch-shaped dumplings out of it. The Arab French girls prepared the vegetables, fruit, and cheese.

"Have they come to the war too?"

"To join their husbands."

"Ours don't take their wives to war," Lara said, "but maybe they should. Then they'd find out what it feels like to die of fear for others."

"Our husbands don't take their wives to war with them either. We're the ones who've come and found them here."

She told Lara how she had met her future husband on the internet. She'd finished high school and was thinking of becoming a nurse, not the kind that works in a hospital, but an emergency nurse, saving the lives of accident victims. She had spent a lot of time at the computer, reading about catastrophes, road and air crashes. She hadn't even noticed how this path had led her into the world of war, to sites devoted to battles, the mujahideen, Palestine, Iraq, Afghanistan, and the jihad. On one of them, she had found an article about a Chechen teenager from a good, well-off family in Amman who had dropped out of medical school to enlist for the war in Syria and to fight as a plain mujahid (though, in Jordan, his father had been a colonel in the Royal Army) in defense of the Syrian Muslims oppressed by the tyrant from Damascus. He had sold his share of the family estate and then used the money to buy medications for the Syrian hospitals. The article was illustrated with photos of the young Chechen, who looked like a fairy-tale prince—tall, with a fine, noble face and sad eyes. She tried to find out more about him, and finally she discovered where to seek news of the mujahideen in Syria and how to get in touch with them. She wrote to him, and he answered. And so their friendship had started. She had never imagined you could fall in love that way. When he wrote and asked if she would come join him and agree to be the wife of a mujahid, she didn't hesitate for an instant. To reassure her parents, she told them she was going to Amman with a girlfriend to visit her family and that she wanted to get to know the Muslim faith and train to be a doctor there. And that they didn't have to pay for anything. After some time, she wrote to tell them she was married. They were angry, especially her father, but she had placated them with a picture of her husband and the news that he was a doctor and a Chechen, although he didn't know a word of the Chechen language.

"I didn't want to lie to them, but I didn't tell them everything either. Because he is a Chechen and a doctor. But they don't know that he's a mujahid," Ayesha said. "He's coming here this evening."

"Did they meet their husbands that way too?"

She nodded.

"They did, and so did all the other girls who come here from Europe for the jihad."

Lara didn't meet Ayesha's husband. He and Shamil and their male friends sat down to supper in the dining room. The women were not allowed to stay in there with them. The girls merely laid the table and then carried in a large tray of fresh, steaming *khinkali* smelling of fresh lamb. Lara smiled, pleased with herself, as she heard the exclamations of delight through the door.

She sat there a while longer, eavesdropping on the sounds of the feast breaking the fast. She thought she could hear Shamil's laughter. She realized that she couldn't remember when he had last laughed as loud. *They're having fun . . . it's good for him*, she thought, but soon chased away that idea.

She was dropping with exhaustion, so she decided to go to bed without waiting any longer for Shamil. But she couldn't sleep. Dull explosions resounded in the distance. Her bedroom was pitch dark—the house had been built with none of the windows looking outside, onto the street. This was to protect the female residents from the stares or accidental glances of strange men. Lara's room had no windows at all, just a second door that opened onto the upper gallery. From there, the horizon wasn't visible, just the sky above the nearby city. She pushed the door open and saw the bright, white flashes of explosions lighting up the darkness. She stepped back inside and then heard a much louder bang, much closer than the previous ones. She froze on the spot, but in minutes, there was another explosion, even closer, and so forceful that Lara felt the floor shaking under her feet. Terrified, she went downstairs, feeling her way in the darkness. The sounds of conversation and laughter were still coming from the sitting room, and the lights were on in the kitchen. There at the table where she and Ayesha had made *khinkali*, the girls in hijabs were staring at a laptop screen.

"Aren't you asleep, girls? Are you watching a movie?" she said.

Embarrassed, they tried to switch off the computer, but she protested.

"Go on watching, please. Why should I mind? I just came down because the explosion frightened me. What on earth was that?"

"A rocket attack, we have them every day," Ayesha replied. "Assad's troops are cowards. They only attack at night, they go for people in their sleep."

Lara peeked at the computer screen.

"What are you watching?"

"*Harry Potter and the Deathly Hallows*, the final part. I've seen it a hundred times before, it helps pass the time while I'm waiting for my husband," Ayesha said. "It's hard to get any new movies here. Honestly, there's nothing much to do . . ."

The next few days went by in the same way, calmly and steadily, as if that was how life would remain forever.

On the first day, she'd jumped in alarm when the muezzin call to prayer roused her from sleep. But then she got used to it. After the early wake-up they prayed, and she went down to the kitchen to make the breakfast, which they ate together before sunrise. During Ramadan, they were allowed their next meal only after dusk.

Until noon, they sat around in the shade of the first-floor gallery talking, reminiscing, or simply gazing at the pond. Shamil told her about his life in Europe and how he had ended up in Syria. It had started with acquaintances he'd struck up at the mosque. There they had often talked about the suffering and injustice faced by Muslims the world over. About Palestine, Kashmir, Bosnia, Chechnya, Afghanistan, and Iraq. They'd also looked at photographs and videos from the wars in those places. Then the war in Syria had erupted, and once again the blood of the faithful was being shed, a whole sea of blood, and the world wasn't lifting a finger to put a stop to it.

First, they had collected money and gifts at mosques for the Syrians. The first time he came to Syria, it was to deliver these donations. The imam from his own mosque had sent him, rather than anyone else, because he spoke Arabic and Turkish, and the journey involved traveling through Turkey to a refugee camp close to the Syrian border.

What he saw there—people's lives destroyed by war, their suffering, and the world's indifference to them—seemed even worse than anything he'd seen earlier on television. As soon as he returned home, he started to consider joining the Syrian insurgents. Finally, when Rustam Gelayev wrote to him from Cairo to say he was dropping out of college and going to the war, Shamil made up his mind and decided to join him. They were going to find each other in Syria, but before he had time to leave Europe, he heard that Rustam was dead, killed in Aleppo right at the start of the major battle for the city.

That same summer, Shamil had gone to Syria too, with three Chechen friends. The imam at their mosque gave them the names, addresses, and phone numbers of people who would help them. They were waiting for them in Gaziantep, just as Shamil's couriers had waited for Lara. Passed from hand to hand, they reached an insurgent camp, where for one hundred days, under the tutelage of emirs seasoned in the Iraq War, they learned to handle weapons, to shoot and fight. They studied military tactics and exercised to develop their strength and endurance. At the camp, he met other Chechens. They teamed up, and after finishing the training course, they joined a unit where some other Chechens were already fighting. Some were from the Caucasus, others were from the Middle East and Europe. They formed their own military force, commanded by Abu Omar. The Chechens were regarded as the best of the insurgents, and the leaders of the insurgency assigned them to the toughest and most important tasks. After several months, Shamil went back to Europe, by the same route Lara had taken to travel to Syria. No one stopped him or asked him any questions—with a European passport in his pocket, he didn't have to worry about visas or border crossings. Before leaving, he resigned from his job at the delivery firm, so on his return from the war he and his wife lived on welfare. A few months later he went to Syria again, and that was when he met the emir, Abu Omar, and become his adjutant and interpreter. This was his fourth time in Syria, and by now he felt entirely at home here.

"Your home is where your family are, your children and your wife," Lara protested.

"I knew you wouldn't understand."

She'd been expecting her remark to upset him; she thought he'd raise his voice, as he always did when they talked about these things, but he replied calmly and even smiled benignly.

"Let's not argue, it's a waste of the time you have here."

She took a close look at him and the life he was leading here in Aleppo, and she could see all too well that now he saw the young men he spent almost all his time with as his closest family. It wasn't that she, his mother, and also his wife and children, had ceased to matter to him, but now other people had come along, these brothers and sisters whom he talked about endlessly. The formerly exclusive and jealously guarded role of those dearest to his heart would have to be shared with them.

There were so many of them! They arrived first thing in the morning and spent all day at the house and in the courtyard. They sat around in the sitting room, hung out in the kitchen, and some of them slept over. They talked, conferred, argued, and laughed. Like at a youth camp during summer vacation, not a war. But there was no adult guardian, no teacher with them. They were their own kings. Emirs. Perhaps that was why they were so bright and cheerful. Maybe they were drunk on the freedom they'd never known in the presence of their elders. At every step, it was plain to see how much they enjoyed this liberty, how much it had gone to their heads. Finally, they felt important, more important and better than their parents or other elders. They'd replaced them in matters those people didn't even dare contemplate, they were fearlessly confronting things that others hadn't the courage to face.

And Shamil, her son, was right in the middle of them all. He was always talking or listening to someone, there was always somebody asking for him, wanting something from him. He was well known for his ability to speak many foreign languages, so they came to him for help; without him, they couldn't communicate. But it was as if he were their leader, guide, and emir. Apart from the time he devoted to her alone, his mother, he was never on his own. She felt grateful to the young people who realized she'd come specially to see him and didn't try to take him away from her.

At noon each day, he left the house for a few hours, as if going to work. He'd say he had to see to some things, because they couldn't cope without him. He'd be back in the early evening. After the first night and the cannonade over the city, Lara begged him not to leave the house after dark. At least not while she was there. He promised, and he kept his word.

He took her for walks around the deserted neighborhood, where they saw large mansions abandoned by their owners. Or they drove the emir's car to the market to buy vegetables, meat for *shashliks*, and mince for *khinkali*. She feared these trips to the bazaar amid the bombed-out houses and burning rubble, but she refused to let him go alone. She usually stayed in the car, watching as he chose tomatoes, cucumbers, onions, and meat. Though one day she walked among the stalls with him. Dusk was gradually falling, and in the ruined district, as in most others, there was no electricity. The vendors had lit oil and kerosene lamps or made bonfires. There was just the occasional lightbulb giving off a green glow, powered by a whirring generator. Among the little stores and stalls teemed a crowd of traders, hemmed in and pawed at by beggars, cripples, and vagabonds. Teenage boys with guns slung across their backs forced their way down the narrow alleys on mopeds.

Lara stepped among these people with her heart on her sleeve. She was afraid that if she went into the crowd and it closed in on her, she'd never emerge again—she'd drown, as in the sea. She kept glancing at Shamil, who was walking just ahead of her. But the crowd didn't push forward or close behind them—instead, it drew aside with solemn respect. At one point, when Shamil stopped at a vegetable stall, an old man came up, kneeled before him, and kissed his hand. Shamil quickly raised him to his feet.

"What was that about?" Lara asked, once they were back in the car with the shopping. "Who was that man?"

"No one. I've never seen him before," Shamil said. "He said he's grateful to us, the mujahideen, for coming to defend them against Assad's men, and that we alone are standing up for them. He said the world has entirely forgotten them, they're dying, but we're the only ones who remember. The West will never be on our side or on the side of the truth," he added. "But soon the time of treachery and exploitation of the true believers will be over. Today we're fighting them for Aleppo, but tomorrow we'll conquer Damascus, Baghdad, and Jerusalem, and then, with God's help, *inshallah*, we'll take Rome. Then the predictions of the Prophet Mohammed will be fulfilled, the blessings and peace of Allah be upon Him, the Antichrist will be defeated and the history of the world will be at an end."

At home he had sometimes told her about the caliphate, the righteous Islamic State that was going to overthrow all existing systems, punish the oppressors and the godless, and restore to the Muslims their former pride and splendor.

"The brothers are coming to join us from all over the world, to win victory together in this last of all wars," he said, listing the countries from which the mujahideen had come. "France, England, Belgium, Germany, Holland, Austria, they're coming from all over Europe, from Africa, even from America and Australia. There are Arabs here, and Uzbeks, our brothers from the Caucasus, and from Russia. There are lots of our people from Chechnya, and from Pankisi too, about a hundred just from the gorge. There are a hundred thousand of us, and there will be more. The whole world is coming here for the war."

He was just as heated as he had been at home, when he'd complained to her that the Kists were ignorant of the word of God and didn't live piously. At the time, she had asked him to stop.

"I can't get my head around it all," she'd said. "I don't want to hear another word."

Before dusk, she made *khinkali* for supper, after which she waited for Shamil to say goodnight to his guests and go to his room. Then she went to bed too. She stood at the door of her son's room, listening to hear if he was asleep. She couldn't help herself. And he was sound asleep, in spite of the din of nocturnal combat that kept her awake.

She went out onto the gallery to look at the sky above the city; there, the distant flashes and muffled roars of exploding missiles reminded her of the storms that rolled through the Caucasian mountains in summer. The order and pace of the day were always the same here, but repeating the same tasks at the same time, and knowing in advance what would happen later, brought her an unexpected sense of calm. *Perhaps the Lord God will be generous and things won't be so bad*, she thought. *Inshallah*.

On the third day, the emir came to visit them in person. Lara was curious about him. This was the man whose orders Shamil was fulfilling, this was her son's superior, on whom his fate depended. If the emir ordered him to die, he'd go to his death without hesitation. But he could spare him too, because he needed him as an interpreter, adjutant, and confidant.

The emir was interested in her too, because he was from the next village in the gorge. He was the same age as Shamil, so they probably went to school together, perhaps in the same grade. But she couldn't remember their being friends; he'd never been to their house, nor had her boys visited him in Birkiani. In his old, prewar incarnation, his name was Tarkhan Batirashvili. She had heard of him, but his fortunes didn't interest her until she discovered that her son had enlisted for the Syrian War and was part of his entourage.

But the insurgent turned herdsman who was also named Omar had known him well. And so had Lara's cousin Ali. A year later, by the campfire at Omar's forest retreat, it was Omar and Ali who told me how the simple shepherd Tarkhan had grown up to be a powerful and sinister emir. By then, his name was known around the world. His enemies saw him as a bloodthirsty, merciless assassin, a criminal threatening international order, and had placed a bounty of millions on his head. But the emir's supporters saw him as an unvanquished warrior, a savior, a new Saladin, a hero, and a future caliph. Every boy in the gorge knows the story of how the humble shepherd boy meta-morphosed into an emir, and every other one of them dreams that Providence will prove as kind to him as it was to Tarkhan from Birkiani.

One day, Ali took me to Birkiani to show me the rundown cottage where the future emir was born and raised. It was on a hillside, far from the main road. Immediately behind it rose a green mountainside. Surrounded by a stone wall, the cottage looked abandoned. There was trash lying around in the yard, and the garden was choked with weeds.

"There's no one here," Ali said, struggling to open the warped, rusty gate. But as soon as it creaked, the door of the cottage opened, and there stood a tall old man in a shabby felt hat. "That's him," Ali said. "Old Batirashvili, Tarkhan's father."

His first name was Teimuraz, and he was an Orthodox Georgian. He had married a local Kist woman who had borne him three sons; Tarkhan was the middle child. Omar remembered him, though, apart from a shock of red hair, he had no special features to distinguish him from the other boys sent from the gorge to help with the cows and sheep. Ali insisted that in those days, Tarkhan had already outstripped his peers in terms of brawn and obstinacy.

"If he made up his mind about something, there was no force on earth that could put him off his plan," he said as we sat around the bonfire.

"He was a good boy, a hard worker, with respect for his elders. He often used to sit by the fire with me, as you are today," Omar agreed, scanning the circle of herdsmen staring at him. "He wasn't the only shepherd from the gorge to become a soldier, anyway. If you happen to be born here, sooner or later you'll end up in a war—if not here, then in Chechnya, Georgia, Abkhazia, or Dagestan. Clearly, Tarkhan was destined for the Syrian one."

He had been called up for military service in the Georgian army. The Kists had always been drawn to soldiering, and for them, army drill and shooting practice brought a pleasant change. Tarkhan enjoyed it so much that he was set on a career in the army. Military service is continual preparation for imaginary wars. But while Tarkhan was in the Georgian army, a real war broke out when Russia invaded Georgia. He wasn't the first or the last Kist to fight against the Russians, but there weren't many who'd been in active combat against them as soldiers in the regular army, rather than as insurgents based in the mountains. The war only lasted five days before the Georgians suffered a resounding defeat, but Tarkhan had proved his valor, cunning, and soldierly skills. He was an excellent shot, and his familiarity with the mountains and the ability to stalk wild animals that he'd gained as a hunter made him a valued scout. Promoted to the rank of sergeant, he dreamed of becoming a lieutenant or captain, and of the resulting salary, which would allow him to feed his family. But he was refused a place at the military academy, and when he fell sick and was diagnosed with tuberculosis, he was discharged from the army as unfit for service.

"That was just idle talk. Don't plenty of people fall sick and then return to perfect health? He was fit as a fiddle and strong as an ox. It wasn't because of sickness that they let him go, it was because he was a Kist, a Chechen. That's how they thanked him for his loyal service. They didn't give him a promotion or a reward, a medal or a pension, they didn't even pay for his medical treatment," Ali said. "That's our fate everywhere. They tell you you're a thief and you'd do better to get yourself a decent job. But if you try to get one, they won't give it to you—they just say you're a thief."

So Tarkhan had gone home to the gorge, but he couldn't find an occupation. He wasn't accepted for the police, and he had no head for business. Finally, to earn a living, he had become involved in smuggling weapons. He was caught and given three years in jail, but there his tuberculosis returned, so they sent him home to avoid infecting the other prisoners.

Before serving time, the future emir hadn't been a religious person. He wasn't raised a Muslim, but an Orthodox Christian, like his father and most other Georgians. He warned his brothers against what he saw as unnecessary religious zeal. But in prison, he underwent a conversion and became an ardent Muslim. His father said that on his first day at home following his release, Tarkhan burned all the family photographs, saying they were a sin against the Creator, as were all pictures, drawings, and sculptures depicting people or animals. Soon after, he packed his bags and informed his father that he was leaving for Turkey. "No one here needs me," he said. But from Turkey, he went straight to Syria, where the civil war had been in progress for a year and where his older brother Tamaz was already living.

It had taken him just a year to rise from a rank-and-file mujahid in the unit of Caucasian volunteers to become its commander, the emir, bearing the adopted name of Abu Omar. He joined the camp of Abu Bakr al-Baghdadi, one of the leaders of the insurgency, who had declared himself the caliph Ibrahim. At the head of his troops, Tarkhan routed the caliph's enemies in Mosul and Fallujah, and the caliph promoted him to be one of his top emirs. Now he had a seat on the Shura Council, which, along with the caliph, was the leading authority in the insurgent state. It was to him, the bravest and most loyal of his emirs, and to his men who had proven themselves in heavy combat, that the caliph entrusted the task of capturing Aleppo.

In those days, no one yet dared cast doubt on the emir's leadership skills, the accuracy of his judgment, his ingenuity, or his wisdom. That was to come later. Many of the officers under his command were to accuse him of caring about nothing but plunder and glory gained through victory at any cost, of treating his soldiers like cannon fodder, sending them to certain death. But at the time Lara was waiting to meet him at the house outside Aleppo, and even a year later, when Ali took me to the emir's family home, he was still being spoken of as a great general and victor. And only his father in the tumbledown cottage resented both the fate that had taken his son away and also his son for leaving him alone in the gorge.

"They say he's a very important emir, one of the leaders of the entire caliphate! Why didn't they appreciate him here in Georgia? Wouldn't such a good soldier have been useful to them? If they'd given him a job, he'd never have gone away, and I wouldn't be living like a beggar now, all on my own in poverty. Is that how an emir's father should live?" old Batirashvili complained as he showed me around the miserable rooms where the only furniture consisted of some metal beds, a table, a few chairs, and a cast-iron stove. "Nowadays, they say he left because of his faith, for the jihad. But I know my facts. He left because he hadn't a kopeck to his name and no prospects in life. If he'd had something to live on, he'd never have gone."

Ali was angry with himself for taking me to the emir's house.

"The old man talks too much. He'd do better to watch his tongue and not blather idle nonsense," he said irritably. "He doesn't deserve to be the father of such a man."

The emir did not arrive until after dusk, for supper, which Lara and the girls had prepared. Lara went upstairs to her bedroom to wait, as she did every day, for the meal to end and Shamil to come find her. She dozed off and didn't hear him knocking at her door. "Your guests are here." Shamil's voice woke her. He was standing in the doorway, as pleased with himself as a child who has played a successful prank. Beside him stood a tall man with a long red beard.

"Mom, this is Abu Omar. That's to say, Tarkhan. I'll leave you alone to have a chat."

Lara didn't know how to behave. Should she do the honors as a hostess, or was she the guest here instead? How was she to address him? Call him by his name or his title? But it looked as if the emir felt awkward too. He seemed reticent and shy, shifting from foot to foot as if he didn't know what to do with himself.

"Straight from Pankisi?" he asked.

"It's a week since I left," she replied with relief.

"How's life at home? What's new in Birkiani?"

He asked about people by name, how they were and what

they were doing. He knew Lara's uncle, who lived in Birkiani, too. He asked about life in the gorge, and she said it was poor, but at least there was no war. He laughed in amusement, but Lara was afraid she might have offended him by saying something inappropriate.

Then she remembered the gift she had brought for the emir at Shamil's request. She fetched her suitcase from under the bed and found the bag of *churchkhela*. She had brought ten pieces and thought it might be too little. But the emir seemed delighted. He immediately broke off a piece and bit into it.

"I'd forgotten how good it tastes," he mumbled.

"It's store-bought, from the bazaar in Duisi. The best is in the fall, when the ingredients are fresh. The nuts, juice, and grapes."

"There's nothing like it here," he said, as if not listening to what she was saying.

They'd been talking for about an hour when she realized that he was awkwardly edging toward the door. He was clearly trying to find the right words to say good-bye.

"You should be proud of your son. He's my right hand, I couldn't manage without him. I have him at my side at all times—where I go, he comes too. And mothers like you are extremely rare as well."

She was afraid he was about to leave, but she hadn't asked him any questions, though there were so many things she wanted him to tell her. What was he planning? What were they planning? What would become of them? She was pleased, she felt pride when he lavished praise on Shamil, saying how much he needed him and what a good mujahid and Muslim he was. Only when he'd gone did it dawn on her what this actually meant—it meant that he wouldn't let her take her son away. He wasn't going to take her side, he wasn't going to support her. He wouldn't tell Shamil to obey his mother, he'd never send him home. So maybe it was a good thing she'd kept quiet.

On the fourth day, somewhere around noon, the house was swarming with visitors. Rows of shoes appeared by the front door, like at the mosque on Fridays before prayers. Army boots, worn-out sports shoes, and sandals. There were animated young men milling around in the hall, the sitting room, and the kitchen. They seemed extremely excited about something, outtalking or, rather, outshouting one another, interrupting one another, and waving their hands around. Lara had wanted to go downstairs, but at the sight of all those unfamiliar men, she retreated back into her room.

She wondered if an important visitor had arrived. If so, he'd come without warning, because if Shamil had known about it, he'd have told her. The young men downstairs seemed very happy—they were congratulating and hugging one another, as if something particularly good and pleasing had happened. Or maybe it was a local holiday?

Through the half-open door, she listened to the sounds from downstairs, trying in vain to catch familiar words, to guess what they were talking about. That afternoon, once the visitors had finally left, she ventured downstairs. Shamil was getting ready to go out too.

"Has something happened? What were all those people doing here?" she asked.

"Yes, something has happened! A great victory! You remember the tower I showed you when we drove to the bazaar?"

She certainly did. He said it was the control tower for a large military air base, from where Assad's planes and helicopters took off for their night raids on Aleppo. He said that for several weeks the mujahideen had been laying siege to the garrison there; they had cut off all its supply routes, but the three thousand soldiers defending the place had resisted storm after storm, and many brothers had been killed.

"But this morning, we managed to break through! Three brothers from Belgium. Just three of them, and they killed a hundred men. What a feat! What a service they've done!"

She didn't understand. Couldn't she tell whom he was talking about? Didn't she know whom he meant by "brothers"?

"Three of our Muslim brothers. They forced their way through the ring of defense and made a breach. Now, God willing, *inshallah*, we'll get inside. We'll take the whole garrison and liberate this brave city. You see, Aleppo has always been against Assad, and now he's punishing it for that."

"How did they force their way through? Just three of them against thousands?"

"They drove a car at full speed between Assad's bunkers and blew themselves up. What a feat! What a service! What joy! And they've become martyrs, *shahideen*. Today they'll rest in the gardens of paradise. How I envy them!"

So that was the reason for the morning's celebrations! Not a victory, but the fact that those three men had been killed. As if their deaths were a reason for joy and pride. Instead of mourning, merriment!

"What are you saying, child?" She raised her hands to her face, as if to shield herself from something. "How on earth? You envy them death?"

"Allah has chosen them. What greater fortune and fulfilment can there be than to sacrifice your life for the faith and for the benefit of others? Every mujahid dreams of it."

"You must live and make the most of your life."

"*Live, live . . . live at any cost . . . it's bound to pay off . . .* That's how the infidels think, and that's why we're going to defeat them. If life were so important, the Almighty would have told us so. Everything here is just of this world; everyone's life here will come to an end, but our real life only starts after death. Every hour, every minute, death is getting nearer. It's not approaching from right or left, or lurking behind us, it's coming straight toward us. And none of us will escape it, we're all destined to stand before the Almighty. What will we say to Him when He asks what we've achieved? We're not here for worldly goods, but to prove our love of God. A mujahid who's prepared to give up his life for the faith and for his maltreated brothers instantly deserves grace and salvation. He will escape the torment of sickness and infirmity, and he'll also have the right to intercede for his loved ones with the Almighty. This is my destiny, this is the path I want to follow to reach Him."

"You're making my head spin."

"I knew you'd find it hard to understand," he said. He came closer and bowed his head. "See that?"

Gently, lovingly, she parted his hair with her fingertips and only now saw a wide, pink scar. He said he'd been wounded. Over a year ago. The two friends he'd been with at the time were killed on the spot—he saw their bodies. They'd become martyrs, *shahideen*, they'd gone to heaven. But he had been taken to a hospital in Turkey. He'd lost a lot of blood, but had survived. He had wanted to die too, to go with his friends. For six hours in the hospital he hadn't allowed the doctors to come near him to dress his wounds. He'd made sure no one gave him any injections or painkillers. All for nothing, because finally he lost consciousness, and they'd saved him.

"And I was so close . . ." He sighed.

"God have mercy," she whispered.

He said he had to go out and would be back later than usual. They were holding an important meeting to discuss the morning's events and make a plan.

"We hardly talk at all," she complained.

"What do you mean? We talk every day. What more do you want to talk about?"

"There are so many things I want to ask you. Somehow, it's not happening . . . Did I tell you I acted in a movie? It's a French one, but it's about our war, in Chechnya . . ."

He promised they'd talk that evening, but he came home with four Chechens from the same town in the Alps where he'd lived with his family. They'd arrived in Syria the previous day by the route Lara had taken. One of the guests was a distant cousin of Shamil's on his father's side. He'd brought him some things from home: a laptop, some clothes, shoes, and a leather jacket. As she was making the supper, she saw her son giving it all away. He only kept the computer. Lara regretted the jacket in particular—it looked new and of good quality. He could have used the shoes as well, because the ones he went about in were almost falling apart. And he had no clothes to speak of. He always wore the same blue shirt and the same baggy pants, which made him look like an Afghan or an Uzbek. Each night, she laundered them for him so they'd be dry by morning and he could put them on clean.

She went upstairs to her room to wait for the guests to leave, then she cleared up after supper, laundered her son's clothes, and hung them out in the courtyard. As she went over their afternoon conversation in her mind, she felt close to despair. There had been occasions before when they didn't agree—they'd argued about hundreds of things. But there had never been such a huge gulf between them before. Maybe that was why they weren't quarreling anymore. For that, you need something that unites you, but now she couldn't keep up with Shamil's notions. In the past, she had known what pleased him, what angered him, and what frightened him. She'd known what it meant when he said he loved or hated. She had loved and hated along with him. Now she couldn't share his emotions with him anymore, she couldn't even identify them. What she regarded as good he regarded as evil, what she saw as white he saw as black, and what he thought a victory was to her mind a defeat. How was she to protect him from his greatest desire in life, the end he longed for at any cost? She understood that human suffering was sometimes so bad that its victims asked to die—anything to be free of it. But why would you go in search of death? She felt as if none of this could really be happening—surely it was just a dream, and any minute now she'd wake up. When she looked at her son, she still saw the same boy, her Shamil. Perhaps it would be enough to grab him by the shoulders, shake him, shout, rouse him, and bring him to his senses. Maybe she'd have to weep and implore him—surely he'd take pity on his mother. *Words are of no use here*, she thought. *God have mercy . . .*

A knock at the door woke her.

"Are you asleep?" he asked.

"I lay down for a bit, and I must have dropped off. Is it so late already? Have they all gone now?"

"No, they're staying the night. But I thought that if you're not too tired, maybe we could talk a while."

"I'm not at all tired." She sat up on the bed, and he settled on the edge of it.

"Mom, when are you thinking of going home?"

She was amazed. She hadn't given any thought to the length of her stay. Her plan was to be here for as long as it took to get him out of the place. Now she knew it'd be harder than she thought, and she'd probably have to stay longer than she imagined.

"Home?"

"I guess you have to get going soon."

"Seven days . . . It was going to be at least seven . . ."

"Things have changed . . . I told you this morning. Our men are going to try to capture the airbase. We don't know what'll happen . . . After that, it might be harder to get out of here . . ."

"When am I to go?"

"Tomorrow would be best . . . The car's coming in the morning with a bodyguard."

"I'm not going anywhere without you . . ."

"You really did come to take me away from here." He smiled in disbelief. "You said you just wanted to say goodbye. Well then, let's say goodbye."

"Did you think I came halfway around the world just to visit you? To this hell? You think I'm going to let you get killed and give you my blessing too? I won't let you throw your life away! I gave it to you, it was me who brought you into this world . . ." She was afraid that if she stopped talking it would be too late, the verdict would be pronounced, and nothing, no love and no words, would ever reverse it. "Think of your own children . . ."

"I have put my life in the hands of God, and in the Holy Koran it says that Allah takes the greatest care of the families of his mujahideen and won't allow any harm to come to them."

"If this were our war, in Chechnya, then I'd understand. To die for your country, fighting against an enemy who's threatening your people . . . But here? In a foreign place? For strangers? This isn't your war. You can't see that they're exploiting you, sending you ahead to your destruction, selling you like slaves. I saw those Arabs in Gaziantep with my own eyes."

"I'm all right here, I've finally found my place, and for the first time I feel truly alive. I'm sorry you don't understand that, because maybe you wouldn't be so worried. I'm not leaving here. I'm never coming back."

"Then I'm staying here with you."

"No, you're not, you can't. The emir has told me to send you back to the border tomorrow. This isn't the time or the place for visitors."

That final night, she couldn't sleep. She lay in darkness, listening to the dull explosions. She only dozed off toward dawn, as the sky was turning gray. When she awoke, Shamil was already up, and two girls whom she hadn't seen before were busy in the kitchen. Outside, the emir's powerful car was waiting, and two more to escort it.

They set off before noon. On the way, they were joined by three more vehicles full of insurgents with guns across their backs.

"You have a retinue like the emir himself," Shamil joked.

In the car, he handed her a bag of provisions that the girls had prepared in the kitchen.

"Those on a journey are excused from fasting."

He said he couldn't give her anything else for the road, not even a few dollars for tickets or water. He had nothing but the shirt on his back and his rifle.

They stopped at the large iron gate. They got out of the car, and he escorted her to the passage across the border. He smiled genially and then stroked her hair through her hijab. She could hardly take in what he was saying.

". . . for what I believe in, and if I'm killed, I'll go straight to heaven. Anyway, maybe I won't die, maybe Allah won't summon me to His side that quickly. Just look at my friend whose house you stayed at. He's been fighting for more than twenty years, he's made a fortune, found a wife and raised a family. It'll be all right, you'll still come to see me and take care of your grandsons."

He went with her to a point where some soldiers were standing. He told her to keep going. Although she was moving and talking, it was as if she were somewhere else, as if it were all happening at a distance. Her mind was a blank, and she felt rising exhaustion, a lack of strength for any enterprise at all, as if she hadn't even the power to raise an objection. The guard held out a hand for her passport. She was almost on the other side; everything was at an end.

"But Shamil . . ." she heard herself say.

And that was the last she saw of him. Once again, she felt weak. They told her to go, to do something, she was being asked questions. But she couldn't speak, or answer any of them.

She had almost no recollection of the journey home, except that everything happened just as it had on the outward journey, but in the opposite direction. Just across the Turkish border, the same courier was waiting for her. He took her to the bus station, bought her a ticket, and put her on the bus. In Istanbul, the next one was waiting. Once again, he took care of everything, paid for everything, and waited for her bus to leave. She let herself be guided and did as they told her, without asking any questions or saying anything.

She slept all the way to the Georgian border. Once on the other side, she finally came to her senses. Maybe it was the sound of Georgian speech that helped her break free of her torpor; for the first time in over a week, at last she could understand what people around her were saying. *Perhaps it'll be all right . . . The guy from Afghanistan has a family and a beautiful house . . . more than twenty years,* she thought. *He'd said, "Finally, I feel truly alive." So maybe he was just saying those things—how like him!—but has no intention of dying at all. It was over her head, but he really did look happy. And they all know and respect him . . . He's a somebody. Maybe God will be generous . . .*

The news that she was back from Syria spread rapidly through the gorge, and at her house in Jokolo, there was a constant stream of unannounced visitors. They were the mothers of boys from Pankisi who had said at home that they were going abroad to work or study but had then been seen in Syria. Now these women were knocking at her door, looking around nervously in case someone saw them and assumed that because they were visiting Lara, their sons must have gone off to the war as well. And then, anxiously sitting at her kitchen table, they asked if perhaps she had seen their Ramzan, Murad, or Beso over there in Syria. Maybe she'd heard something? Maybe someone had mentioned them . . . *Abu, a tall, skinny boy, with a wide scar from his nose to his jaw following a fight with some Georgian boys from Matani, one of whom had slashed his face with a knife.* Had she seen him? No? *Maybe you saw my boy, Isa? He knew your sons, he came to your house once.* Lara had had no idea so many young men from the gorge had gone to Syria and enlisted for the war. Maybe if she'd known that sooner, she would have asked more questions and kept her ears open. But yes, she'd only tried to bring her own son home with her.

On the fourth day after her return from Aleppo, she went to Telavi to do some shopping. Her phone rang just as she was walking among the market stalls. The number that showed up on the screen wasn't local, and she knew at once it was from abroad. It was Rashid, her younger son, calling.

"Shamil has gone," he said in a sad, muted tone. "He's dead. Our Shamil has become a martyr, a *shahid*."

All Lara can remember is that she put her phone back in her purse. She woke up in the hospital. The doctor told her she had fainted and hit the back of her head on the sidewalk. It was very dangerous, he warned. He advised her to be careful not to make any sudden movements for the next few days, not to lift anything at all, and to avoid strong emotions. He asked if anything like this had ever happened to her before. He said he could give her an injection to boost her strength and she'd feel better right away, but she replied that she didn't want any injections. And then she burst into tears as she remembered that Shamil hadn't wanted any injections either—he'd just wanted to be allowed to die in peace.

She remained in the hospital for two weeks. When the doctors found out what had happened to her, they refused to let her go home in a hurry, but felt it better for her to stay in their care for a while. As soon as she got home, she sent Rashid a message to say that she must speak to him urgently. Lately, they hadn't spoken as often as in the past. She told herself he was an adult, with his own family, his own problems, and his own life. It was enough for her to be sure she knew where to find him and that she could contact him at any moment.

Rashid showed up that same night. She barely recognized him. He had a long beard and a shaven skull. She thought he'd shaved his head as a sign of mourning for his brother, but the beard worried her—it was too similar to the ones worn by the mujahideen in Chechnya, Pankisi, and Aleppo. Shamil had told her that Rashid had been to Syria twice as well and had fought in the war. Shamil was very proud of Rashid. The mujahideen in Aleppo called him a *hafiz*, a "Guardian of the Book." That was the title conferred on those who knew the Koran inside out, retained it in their memory, and were able to recite it beautifully. Crowds came to Rashid's recitations. The brothers had jointly decided that they'd take turns going to Syria and that if one of them were killed, the other would take care of their families.

"Shamil has gone. What are your plans?"

"I should do what he has done, I should follow his path. It was my dream too."

But when Lara began to cry, he promised he wouldn't go back to the war.

"Forgive me, I don't want you to suffer. Don't worry, I'll take care of you, I won't leave you on your own."

"You haven't a choice. You're all I have left. They don't take only sons into the army, and even the emirs don't let them join the insurgents."

Rashid promised to do as she wished. A few days later, he called again and told her Shamil had been killed at night, straight after the battle for Menagh Airbase, which the mujahideen had finally taken. Rashid had seen a photograph of his brother on the internet, standing in an aircraft hangar beside a captured plane. It looked as if the picture had been taken shortly before he died. He also said that the battle for the airbase had prompted a quarrel among the Caucasian mujahideen commanders. Those who had fought together in Chechnya earlier on kept close company in Syria too, and they looked down on those like Shamil, and even emir Abu Omar, who hadn't taken part in the war in the Caucasus. After the attack on the airbase, the Chechen veterans had accused emir Abu Omar of needlessly losing dozens of men during the fighting, sending them into the storm the way a sultan would send in his

Janissaries. They had marched on the enemy trenches over the corpses of their comrades.

Rashid called several times more, and once or twice he appeared on Lara's computer screen too. And then he fell silent—he simply disappeared. She sat it out for two weeks and then called, although they had agreed that he would get in touch with her. He didn't pick up the call. She waited a month, but nothing changed.

At the time, when he called with the news of his brother's death, she had felt a sense of threat, but her despair at losing Shamil had used up her remaining strength and dulled her intuition. When first told that Shamil had gone to the war in Syria, she'd been horrified and had refused to believe it. But when it turned out to be true, she knew that her younger son would soon follow his brother. They'd always been inseparable, where one went, so did the other, as if they couldn't live without each other. And that really was the case. They were each other's only source of support.

Finally, she tried calling every day, but Rashid didn't answer. His wife reassured her, saying one time that he was away on business, another time that he'd gone to visit friends. During one of these conversations, gripping the phone tightly, Lara suddenly felt certain she'd lost her second son too.

"I know he's in Syria," she told her daughter-in-law. "People have seen him there."

Lara was bluffing, but she had to know the truth.

The girl burst into tears. "Yes, it's true, he's gone," she admitted.

After returning from Aleppo, Lara had half expected the news of Shamil's death. Once she was sure that Rashid had gone to the war in Syria too, she knew he would be killed as well. Unless she saved him.

She resolved to go back to Aleppo, to find the emir and, with his help, find Rashid too. And she wouldn't return to the gorge without him. She'd heard that in Azerbaijan, Dagestan, Kabardia, and Russia, those who'd been to fight in Syria were sent to prison, and only then did they come home from the war. An equivalent law was being drafted in Georgia. In Chechnya, it was announced that the parents and brothers of those who went to the Syrian war would be punished in their place, and their family homes would be razed. *Let him go to jail, at least he'll be safe there. Anything's better than death*, Lara thought. *Anyway, maybe his European passport will protect him and they'll set him free sooner. After all, he's a European!*

She called Rashid's wife again. She told her to tell Rashid she knew the truth and that he was to get in touch with her immediately. All the stress and worry made her ill again, and she landed in the hospital in Tbilisi.

The phone rang during a ward round, so she couldn't answer it, but she glanced at the screen and recognized her daughter-in-law's number. An hour later she called again.

"How are you feeling?" the young woman asked. "There's something I have to tell you."

"You don't have to tell me anything! I don't want to know!" Lara cried and hurled the phone away from her, smashing it to pieces.

She had lost Rashid . . .

But she couldn't imagine his death. Sometime later, she learned that it had happened during combat on the outskirts of Aleppo. The insurgents had lost this particular skirmish. Following a failed attack on Assad's prison, they had retreated, with the Syrian army in pursuit. She was told that Rashid had rushed to the aid of his commander, who was trapped and under fire in one of the buildings.

Some said Rashid had been hit by a sniper's bullet before managing to reach the commander's hiding place. Others had seen him run inside, but moments later, the whole building had exploded, hit by an artillery shell. Or perhaps as he ran among the ruins, Rashid had set off a hidden mine?

No one had seen him since, and his body was never found. Nobody had searched for him in the rubble or checked to see if he was wounded but alive, to be brought out from under fire and transported to a military hospital. The entire district, along with the dead and wounded, was soon captured by government troops.

"They didn't even recognize him as a martyr, one of the *shahideen*. Nobody was sure if he'd been killed, and they couldn't see him as a hero like Shamil. They didn't even add his name to the honor roll, or bury him in a special grave."

I could hear a note of resentment in Lara's voice, as if she had a grudge against fate for the wrong that had been done to her younger son, as if she thought he hadn't been treated fairly by being excluded from the company of martyrs.

"Though he fought and was killed like his older brother." Unexpectedly, she smiled, a touch ironically, a touch sadly, as if aware of her own inconsistency. After all, she'd done everything she could to keep both her sons off that honor roll, but now she was sorry Rashid's name wasn't on it. That's life! "In life they were always together. Only death separated them. They both used to say that when they died they'd go to the same place and that unimaginably beautiful *houris* would come for them at the hour of their death to show them the way to paradise, so maybe it's all true . . ."

For a time, she went on hoping for a call from Europe or from Aleppo, announcing that by some miracle Rashid was still alive. But he never called again. Several weeks later, the wallet he had left behind before the battle was sent back from Syria. In it were a handful of banknotes, some documents, and a notebook with phone numbers and addresses—all that was left of him.

For a while she nodded her head in the sparing, economical gesture of someone who hasn't much strength and must use it carefully to avoid running out of it too soon. For a long time, neither of us spoke, and I figured our conversation had reached its end. Then, suddenly, she leaned toward me across the table as if she had an important final message to convey to me.

"They haven't entirely gone." She smiled knowingly, as if after everything I'd heard, she wanted to console me. "I switch on my computer at night, and I watch them. I know just where to look and how to make them show up on my screen as they used to. First Rashid. He's sitting on the couch at his place in Europe. But he's not looking at me. His eyes are closed. He's reciting the Koran by heart, which sounds like singing, like one of our songs from the Caucasus, sad and full of yearning. Rashid sings beautifully, I could listen to him for hours, although I can't understand a word. He must have inherited his voice and his ear for music from me. And my youngest grandson is sitting on his knee. He's a little monkey! He's teasing his father, pulling his beard. And he's looking at me, as if showing off to me, not the camera.

"Shamil is emerging from an orange grove outside the house in Aleppo. The house is visible too, but only just, behind a wall in the background. It was only here that I took a close look at Shamil and saw how gaunt he was. He probably hadn't fully recovered yet from that head wound. When I was there with him, somehow I didn't really notice—my thoughts were otherwise engaged. Shamil, Shamil . . . Sometimes I watch him, and it feels as if he's about to say, 'Momma, your guests are here,' just as usual. Then someone asks him to say something, to summon the brothers to fight. At first he speaks quite calmly, but then he gets more heated, talking louder and louder and waving his hands around . . . so like him. At first I couldn't understand a word of it because it was all in Arabic, but then I found a translation into Russian. He was recruiting others for the war, summoning them to come to Syria and not hide from death, because no one will escape it anyway. When I watch him doing that, I'm filled with the desire to say, 'I don't want to listen to that, stop it.'"

Lara wanted to go back to the outskirts of Aleppo again to stand by Shamil's grave and at least see the place where Rashid was killed. She found a way to write to the emir Abu Omar, whose interpreter and adjutant Shamil had been. But he had a message sent to her to say that he didn't agree with her plan.

"He had them tell me I had nothing to look for there. And that there's no point in dwelling on the past or depriving the dead of peace. You must live, not die. That's what he had them tell me."

* * *

Lara regularly visits the small town in the Alps where Shamil and Rashid once lived and where they left their families, their widows and six children. Her sons' father, her former husband, lives there too. They've never divorced, but they've never reunited either, ever since the war separated them in Grozny. They haven't even tried; they simply ceased to exist for each other. Lara doesn't know how her husband lives or what he does. She hasn't even spoken to him since their sons' deaths. And she doesn't want to talk about him.

The first time she went to the Alpine town was a year after her sons' deaths. She wanted to meet her grandsons. They were the first in the family not to be born in the Pankisi Gorge or the Caucasus, but in Europe—the first Europeans in the family.

She took them for walks in the streets of the town where, instead of Caucasian highlanders, her sons were supposed to have become Europeans, citizens of a better world. She examined the people, the houses, and the parks, trying to fathom what it was about this place that had changed her sons. One day, she heard Kheda, Shamil's wife, talking about the brothers in faith, the caliphate, and the jihad. At first, Lara thought she had misheard, but a few days later the girl was talking about martyrs, the *shahideen* again, saying that she herself would be willing to follow in her husband's footsteps.

Since then, Lara has traveled to the Alps each year for several months at a time. She leaves at the end of winter, when the weather improves and it's easier for her elderly parents to manage without her. She goes back in the fall, when the Kists start heading into the mountains to gather sweet chestnuts that they'll sell for a pittance to the dealers from Azerbaijan and Turkey who drive into Duisi in huge trucks.

She has never understood what happened to Shamil and Rashid. Perhaps at the time when we met, she already knew that she'd never understand it, but she figured that if she were present in her grandsons' lives, if she kept an eye on them, in some way, by being there, she could oppose the incomprehensible force that had taken away her sons.

She hadn't dropped the idea of setting up a guesthouse for foreign hikers, and was planning to involve Omar from the mountains and her cousin Ali in the enterprise. Ali was approaching forty and couldn't earn the money to maintain his family in the gorge. He'd even been to Syria and enlisted in the war, but had come home six months later. Now he was bored in the village, complaining that he had nothing to occupy him. He spent his time in the mountains with Omar, where he sat by the campfire, telling the herdsmen about the war and showing them short videos recorded on his phone in Syria and featuring insurgent parades, army drills, shooting practice, the chaos of combat, shouts of *Allahu akbar*, and the mutilated bodies of his fallen comrades. The young shepherds couldn't tear their eyes off him. As they listened, they moved their lips in silence, as if repeating every word, as if wanting to make his story their story, the things he'd seen and experienced their fate too.

One night, Ali saw a friend of his fifteen-year-old son among his listeners. The next day, he came running to Lara.

"Another year or two, and my boy will end up like me, or like your sons," he said.

Ali tried to leave for Europe with his family as a refugee. Somewhere he'd heard that to mark an important holiday, Germany was accepting anyone who wanted to settle there, as long as they arrived by a fixed deadline. Lara tried to explain that this was how swindlers fooled people into traveling abroad, so they could buy their houses and farms at half price. But Ali wouldn't listen. He didn't sell his house, but he borrowed money from the neighbors for the journey. He wasn't allowed to enter Europe, so he returned to the gorge and started to consider leaving for the war in Syria again. Lara told him that if that was his plan, he might as well take his son with him right away—they might as well die together, then at least neither would have to weep for the other. He promised not to go, but said he'd look around for work in Tbilisi or Baku instead. Lara felt sure he would, and believes she managed to save his life.

In our conversations, she liked to go back to the French movie in which she acted for a world-famous director. I didn't want to tell her that although the movie was selected to compete for the Palme d'Or, its original version was panned by the critics and got scathing reviews, though it was later improved. It was dubbed the most agonizing flop of the season, a terrible piece of kitsch. The critics accused the director of creating central characters that weren't at all credible and whose actions and motives were unclear. The whole thing was tediously full of cheap tricks and affectation. "The picture of indigence and despair," one of the reviewers wrote.

Lara would have been disappointed.

Author's Note

Lara is not the real name of the woman at the center of this story. At her request, I have changed it, along with the names of most of the other people who feature in this book.

In October 2018, *All Lara's Wars* was published in translation into Georgian and launched at Lara's house in her home village of Jokolo.

My thanks to Marcin Zaremba.

A Time Line of Events at the Tumultuous Turn of the Twenty-first Century

1991   Economic and political decline lead to the collapse of the Soviet Union, the communist mutation of tsarist Russia. One after another, the Soviet Empire's conquered territories declare independence. One of the first to do so, before the formal break-up of the empire, is Georgia. In revenge, and to defend its dominions to the last, Russia incites the dependent Georgian provinces of Abkhazia and South Ossetia to rebel against Georgia. Only days after Georgia's declaration of independence, a ruinous, fratricidal civil war erupts. In the fall, following the example of other conquered territories, Chechnya declares independence from Russia too. Russia, which, with no alternative, has recognized the independence of the other territories that formed the Soviet Union, refuses to acknowledge Chechnya's autonomy, claiming that it was not a Soviet Republic as Georgia, Uzbekistan, and Belarus were, but part of Russia itself. But the main reason for Russia's objection is the Kremlin's concern that agreeing to Chechnya's independence will prompt an avalanche of withdrawals, and that the Tatars, Bashkirs, Buryats, Yakuts, Kalmyks, Avars, Lezgins, and Circassians will all follow the

Chechen example and demand their own autonomy, which will lead to the disintegration not just of the Russian Empire (of which the Soviet Union was the final incarnation), but of Russia itself.

The fall of communism and the end of the Cold War era prompt many Western leaders to declare the ultimate victory of free-market liberalism. In response to the Iraqi army's attack on Kuwait and its oil fields, the United States, the last world superpower, invades Iraq, landing its troops in Saudi Arabia.

1993 Civil war erupts in Afghanistan among the mujahideen, who in the 1980s caused the Soviet army heavy losses, hastening the bankruptcy of the Soviet Union and communism. Muslim volunteers, thousands of whom have arrived in Afghanistan for the holy war, are disappointed by the querulous, small-minded Afghans and leave the Hindu Kush mountains. They return to their countries of origin, where they try to incite and wage their own holy wars (in Algeria, for instance, and Sudan) or enlist for other wars involving Muslims (in the Balkans and in Kashmir). The uncrowned king of the "knights of the holy war," the Saudi millionaire Osama bin Laden, regards the presence of American troops in Saudi Arabia as a desecration of the fatherland of the Prophet and declares war on the West.

1994 In deep crisis, Russia decides to send an armed punitive expedition to the Caucasus to crush the Chechens, who have declared independence. The invasion is a fiasco and develops into a long and bloody guerrilla war that attracts Muslim volunteers from the Middle East to the Caucasus in support of the Chechens.

1996 Failing to beat the Chechens, Russia signs a cease-fire, which is regarded as a victory for the insurgents. The Kremlin agrees to postpone the issue of Chechnya's status for five years. In Chechnya, as in Afghanistan, the victorious insurgents quarrel and fight one another for power. Opponents of the insurgent authorities appeal to Islam to win themselves the aid of super-rich Arab sheikhs from the Persian Gulf.

In Afghanistan, the civil war is won by the Taliban, radical Muslims who take power in Kabul. Not recognized by the world (except for Pakistan, Saudi Arabia, and the United Arab Emirates), they are the only authorities to give official recognition to Chechnya's independence. At the Taliban's invitation, Osama bin Laden, with warrants issued for his arrest, settles in Afghanistan and establishes the headquarters of his international terrorist organization, Al Qaeda, in the Hindu Kush.

1999 Without waiting for the five-year truce to elapse, Russia invades Chechnya again, claiming that under its rebel governments, it has become a den of world-threatening jihadists, terrorists, and human traffickers. This time, insurgents from groups that invoke Islam and slogans of the holy war are dominant within the Chechen resistance movement. The Russian military mission is commanded by the previously unknown Vladimir Putin, who, to the surprise of many, is promoted to the post of prime minister. Toward the end of the year, the Russians win the high-speed war, in which this time they have avoided ground battles, applying a scorched-earth strategy instead. The victory brings Putin both great popularity and the presidency, left vacant by the forced resignation of his predecessor, the ailing and unpopular Boris Yeltsin.

In the Middle East, Osama bin Laden makes war on the reviled West. His supporters blow up the U.S. embassies in Kenya and Tanzania and attack American targets in the Middle East. In the Balkans, the last of the local wars erupts in Kosovo, where the West gives military support to the Kosovan Albanians against Serbia, Russia's ally. Russia regards this as treachery on the part of the West. Muslim volunteers, who earlier supported the Muslims in Bosnia, fight on the Kosovan side too.

2001 With Osama bin Laden's blessing, terrorists kidnap commercial passenger planes and use them to attack New York City and Washington. In retaliation, the United States invades Afghanistan, where the international terrorist organization Al Qaeda has established its headquarters.

In the Caucasus, the Chechen insurgents routed by

the Russians hide in the mountains and travel across to neighboring Georgia, which has not yet recovered from the decline following the civil wars of its first few years of independence. The West, which until now has sympathized with the Chechens, turns its back on them because it has a greater need of Russia's help in the third world war known as the "war against terrorism." With no support from the West, the Chechen insurgents join the jihadist camp in ever greater numbers.

2003 Wishing to bring pro-Western order to the Middle East, and to guarantee their own security, the United States and its Western allies invade Iraq, falsely accusing the Iraqi tyrant Saddam Hussein of building nuclear weapons and of supporting bin Laden's terrorist organization. The American notion is of a new order in Iraq to serve as an example to other Muslim countries in the Middle East.

The West regards the Afghan war as a victory at last and transfers its troops, money, and entire focus to the Middle East. The Afghan Taliban take advantage of this to rebuild their insurgent army and attack Afghanistan from the border with Pakistan.

In Georgia, the "Rose Revolution" occurs in the streets of Tbilisi with Western support, ousting the weak, corrupt government and promoting in its place politicians who declare themselves pro-Western. The Georgian revolution is modeled on the one that took place earlier in Belgrade, which deposed Serbia's president, who was hostile to the West. In the wake of the Rose Revolution, similar street revolutions, also backed by the West, take place in Ukraine and Kyrgyzstan, bringing down the governments in those countries and empowering factions that favor integration with the West. Russia regards the "color revolutions" as a hostile act by the West, an attempt at political interference in territories that the Kremlin has not ceased to regard as its own exclusive sphere of influence.

The Caucasian insurgents more frequently and readily apply terrorist tactics. In 2002, they attack the Dubrovka Theater in Moscow and take hostages to force Russia to withdraw its troops from Chechnya. In 2004 they carry out a similar terrorist raid on a school in Beslan, North Ossetia.

2006 Instead of being a victorious high-speed war, the American invasion of Iraq morphs into a long and violent occupation. Muslim volunteers pour into Iraq from all over the world to enlist in the holy war against the Americans. In the Iraqi desert, a local branch of Al Qaeda is formed, though previously not present here. It is joined by battle-seasoned soldiers from the ousted Hussein's army, which the Americans have dissolved. Gradually, the Iraqi branch of Al Qaeda becomes increasingly independent of the central command, and finally regards itself as a separate group known as Islamic State.

2007   When the Russians kill Aslan Maskhadov, the Chechen president who led the fight for autonomy, the Caucasian insurgents give up the fight for Chechnya's independence, but they declare the Caucasus an Islamic emirate and announce their intention of joining Al Qaeda.

2008   In response to promises made by the West to admit Georgia to its military and economic alliances, Russia provokes and wins a five-day border war against Georgia, routs the local army, and officially recognizes the rebel provinces of Abkhazia and South Ossetia as independent countries.

2009   Barack Obama, the new president of the United States, declares an end to the American wars instigated by his predecessor in Afghanistan and Iraq and promises to restore friendly relations with Russia.

2011   In the Middle East, the Arab Spring occurs, leading to the deposing of the dictators ruling Tunisia, Egypt, Lebanon, and Yemen, all of whom were on good terms with the West. In Syria, the local dictator refuses to yield to urban riots, and civil war erupts nationwide.

    After eight years at war, the American troops vacate Iraq, leaving behind in Baghdad a government dominated by Shi'ites, who represent the majority of the country's population. Though complaining of persecution, the Sunnis declare their allegiance to Baghdad, but the Iraqi branch of Al Qaeda, now named Islamic State, takes action in their name and defense. The civil war in Syria increasingly acquires the character of a conflict between the Sunnis and the ruling coalition of Shi'ites, Alawites, and Christians, regarded by their enemies as infidels and traitors.

In Pakistan, Osama bin Laden is killed by American commandos, and Al Qaeda, its members deprived of leadership and hunted down, is decimated by the Americans and gradually loses significance among jihadists.

2013　In Iraq, an armed Sunni insurgency erupts, led by Islamic State. Its soldiers are also fighting in neighboring Syria, where the West, battered by the wars in Afghanistan and Iraq, and in deep economic recession, is unable to force the warring sides to reach a truce or to protect the civilian population from slaughter. It is estimated that by now almost a quarter of a million people have died in the Syrian war. Thanks to the helplessness and passivity of the West, Muslim volunteers from all over the world, including the West, head for Syria. From Europe alone, some fifteen thousand Muslims who hold European passports, the offspring of political and economic migrants, enlist for the Syrian war. Unable to stand up to the Russian army, insurgents from the Caucasus also leave for Syria.

2014　With its thousands of volunteers, its combat fitness, and the armaments it has captured from the Iraqi army

(American weapons) and the Syrian army (Soviet and Russian weapons), Islamic State takes the lead in the civil wars in Iraq and Syria. The jihadists invalidate the border between Iraq and Syria, and in the territory under their control (one third of Iraq and more than half of Syria), they declare the establishment of a caliphate, with its own terrain, government, laws, courts, police, and army. It is headed by the leader of Islamic State, Abu Bakr al-Baghdadi, who regards himself as the caliph Ibrahim. The caliphate declares its branches in Nigeria, the Maghreb countries (in North Africa), Afghanistan, Pakistan, and Central Asia. The small number of insurgent commanders still fighting in the Caucasus declare their readiness to join the caliphate too.

After a thirteen-year war, the longest in U.S. history, the United States and its Western allies withdraw their troops from Afghanistan.

In Kiev, another street revolution, supported by the West, overthrows Ukraine's pro-Russian government and brings to power politicians who favor integration with the West. Russia responds by annexing Crimea and by supporting Russian separatists who incite an armed uprising in Eastern Ukraine. President Putin, who started his career by winning the war in Chechnya, declares that the Kremlin claims the right to military intervention anywhere in the world where the rights and liberty of Russians are under threat.

2015 The expansion of the caliphate, which now rules over almost ten million people, means that first the Americans and soon after their Western and Arab allies, including France, the United Kingdom, Australia, Saudi Arabia, the United Arab Emirates, Bahrain, Qatar, and Jordan, launch air attacks against the one-hundred-thousand-strong jihadi army. The aim of this airborne assistance is to stop the victorious advance of the caliphate army and also to reinforce the pro-Western insurgent troops fighting against Syrian president Bashir al-Assad. In revenge, the jihadis launch suicide bomb attacks in major Western cities, including Paris (2015); Nice, Brussels, and Berlin (2016); and London and Manchester (2017). Russia also becomes involved in the Syrian war, joining Iran and Hezbollah (the Lebanese "Army of God") on Assad's side. At first Russia sends only its air force to Syria, but shortly after, Russian instructors land at the post-Soviet military base at Tartus, on the Mediterranean, which Russia has leased for another fifty years. With them come veterans of the Russian invasions of Crimea and the Donbass, recruited by the private security firm the Wagner Group, which provides services to the Kremlin; and also Chechen soldiers, sent by Ramzan Kadyrov, the Chechen leader raised to power in Grozny by Putin and staunchly loyal to him. Kadyrov's men have taken part in previous Russian military expeditions in Georgia and also in Ukraine.

2016   Iraqi government troops supported by the Americans launch a counterattack on the jihadis in Iraq, while with the help of Russia, Iran, and Hezbollah, the Syrian army launches one in Syria. Toward the end of the year, the Syrian army captures Aleppo.

2017   In the summer, Iraqi troops take Mosul, and in the fall, Syrian and Kurdish insurgent units supported by the United States and its Western allies drive the jihadis out of their capital in the Syrian city of Raqqa.

2018   After breaking up the caliphate, the Russians and Americans, the former supporting the Syrian authorities and the latter the opposition, set about fighting for influence in Syria and the Middle East. At the beginning of the year, Russian mercenaries recruited by the Wagner Group and fighting for a salary and a commission from the Syrian oil fields captured for Russian oil companies, mistakenly attack an American base in the nearby desert city of Deir ez-Zur, close to the Iraqi border. The Americans repel the attack, decimating the attackers. About a hundred Russian mercenaries are killed in the nighttime battle, and as many are wounded. Lasting for several hours, the desert battle, though accidental and indirect, is regarded as the first armed clash of the superpowers as rivals for dominance since the Second World War kept the world in a state of cold war for almost half a century. Fought according to cold war rules, the surrogate war in Syria ends in a win for Russia. Her protégé, President Assad, retains power and regains control of the Syrian state, and thanks to its military and political successes, Russia regains its status as a global superpower.

2019 In February, whether consciously lying or with no knowledge of the actual state of affairs, Donald Trump (who in 2017 succeeded Barack Obama as president of the United States) announces ultimate victory over the caliphate. In fact, the war continues until the end of March, when the insurgents allied with the West capture the caliphate's final stronghold in the town of Baghuz, on the eastern bank of the Euphrates River.

Translator's Glossary

abrek: A North Caucasian term that in Chechen means "avenger," but that was used as a propaganda term for insurgents fighting the Soviets after the Second World War, who were popularly regarded as defenders of the motherland.

aul: A word of Turkic origin for a fortified village in the Caucasus. *Auls* were built of stone, often against cliffs. The *auls* of the Svaneti region in Georgia, with their distinctive fortified towers, are a World Heritage Site.

churchkhela: A popular Georgian candy made of grape must, nuts, and flour, sometimes also with chocolate and raisins. The nuts and other solid ingredients are strung together on fishing line or string and dipped in corn flour and thickened grape juice, then dried in the shape of candles.

emir: Arabic for prince or aristocrat, but also for a military commander.

hafiz: Arabic for a person who has memorized the entire Koran.

houri: Arabic for the beautiful virgins who, in Islamic belief, will welcome the faithful to paradise.

iftar: Arabic for the evening meal with which Muslims end their daily Ramadan fast at sunset.

jihad: Arabic for "striving" or "struggling," especially with a praiseworthy aim; it has come to be used in English to mean "the holy war," "the crusade."

khinkali: Georgian dumplings made with various fillings, including minced meat, onions, herbs, and spices.

madrassa: Arabic for an educational institution, secular or religious. In English, it is generally used to refer to a school or college for the study of Islam.

mujahid: (plural: *mujahideen*) Arabic for a person engaged in jihad; originally used in English to refer to the guerrilla-type military groups led by the Islamist Afghan fighters in the Soviet-Afghan War and used now to describe other jihadist groups in various countries.

mullah: A Muslim who is educated in Islamic theology and religious law.

Salafi: A reform branch of Sunni Islam that supports the implementation of sharia (Islamic) law.

shahid: (plural: *shahideen*) Arabic for "witness"; also used to mean "martyr."

sheikh: Arabic honorific used not just for royalty, but also for a leader, elder, or noble.

stanitsa: Russian or Ukrainian for a village within a Cossack "host," a territory settled by Cossacks, who were obliged to provide a military force for the imperial Russian army, largely to protect the borders.